Meditations On Holy Week

Anthony J Kelly CSsR

Meditations On Holy Week

The Scandal of the Cross

Anthony J Kelly CSsR

Foreword by Archbishop Mark Coleridge

Adelaide
2023

Text copyright © 2023 remains with the Anthony J Kelly and the CSsR, Australia, and for the collection with ATF Theology. All rights reserved. Except for any fair dealing permitted under the Copyright Act, no part of the publication may be reproduced by any means without prior permission. Inquiries should be made in the first instance with the publisher.

A Forum for Theology in the World
Volume 10, Issue 2, 2023

A Forum for Theology in the World is an academic refereed journal aimed at engaging with issues in the contemporary world, a world which is pluralist and ecumenical in nature. The journal reflects this pluralism and ecumenism. Each edition is theme specific and has its own editor responsible for the production. The journal aims to elicit and encourage dialogue on topics and issues in contemporary society and within a variety of religious traditions. The Editor in Chief welcomes submissions of manuscripts, collections of articles, for review from individuals or institutions, which may be from seminars or conferences or written specifically for the journal. An internal peer review is expected before submitting the manuscript. It is the expectation of the publisher that, once a manuscript has been accepted for publication, it will be submitted according to the house style to be found at the back of this volume. All submissions to the Editor in Chief are to be sent to: hdregan@atf. org.au.

Each edition is available as a journal subscription, or as a book in print, pdf or epub, through the ATF Press web site — www.atfpress.com. Journal subscriptions are also available through EBSCO and other library suppliers.

Editor in Chief
Hilary Regan, ATF Press

A Forum for Theology in the World is published by ATF Theology and imprint of ATF (Australia) Ltd (ABN 90 116 359 963) and
is published twice or three times a year.

ISBN:	
	978-1-923006-80-5 soft
	978-1-923006-81-2 hard
	978-1-923006-82-9 epub
	978-1-923006-83-6 pdf

Published by

THEOLOGY

Making a lasting impact

An imprint of the ATF Press Publishing Group
owned by ATF (Australia) Ltd.
PO Box 234
Brompton, SA 5007
Australia
ABN 90 116 359 963
www.atfpress.com
Making a lasting impact

A Forum for Theology in the World Vol 10 No 2/2023

Table of Contents

Foreword		vii
Archbishop Mark Coleridge		
1.	St Paul and the Cross	1
2.	Jesus Washes the Disciples Feet	13
3.	The Last Supper	19
4.	The Eucharist and Ecology	27
5.	Via Dolorosa: The Pathway to Calvary	31
6.	Good Friday	41
7.	Befriending Death	47
8.	Holy Saturday: The Longest Day	55
9.	The Empty Tomb	65
10.	He is Risen	69
11.	Toward the Ascension	81
12.	The Glory of God	89

A Forum for Theology in the World Vol 10 No 2/2023

Foreword

The story of Holy Week is very familiar, too familiar perhaps. Its events, characters and images are so embedded in our culture, even in our language, that it can be simply taken for granted, leaving us thinking that we know all there is to know about the story of Jesus' passion, death and resurrection. The story has lost much of its power to shock us and to illumine the dark reaches of the human soul. This is supremely true of the Cross, the utter strangeness of which is lost on a culture in which it has become a conventional symbol of religious respectability. Yet this was not so for the early Christians who shared the Roman world's abhorrence of crucifixion. So great was their sense of shock that Jesus, the Son of God, should end up a corpse on a Cross that they refrained for centuries from representing it visually. It was simply too confronting.

In the meantime the Cross of Jesus and the story of Holy Week have become so familiar that we need a kind of defamiliarisation if we are to recover a sense of shock and astonishment at what the story reveals, if we are to see it with new eyes and understand it with new minds. In these meditations, Anthony J Kelly CSsR offers that kind of defamiliarisation, in order to see and understand Holy Week, its events, its characters, its images, in new ways. As the meditations unfold, you can sense Fr Kelly's own astonishment at what is happening and what it means; and into this astonishment he invites the reader. He leads us far beyond 'just another Holy Week' to a new experience of Holy Week, almost as if for the first time. The all too familiar appears in all its strangeness; and as it does a sense of astonishment emerges.

This is like the amazement of which Pope John Paul II wrote in his first Encyclical Letter, *Redemptor Hominis*. There he claimed that Christianity is not really a conventional religion: it is an experience. It is an experience of encounter with the crucified and risen Christ; and in that encounter we see the full and magnificent truth of who God really is, who the human being really is and how the two relate. That vision becomes an experience of amazement; and that amazement, says the Pope, is Christianity (10). Tony Kelly's meditations in these pages lead us through the story of Holy Week, with all its darkness, into that experience of amazement.

Normally it is poets, musicians and artists who specialise in the art of defamiliarisation, leading us to see in new and revelatory ways what we know without really knowing. Here however it is a systematic theologian, though Tony Kelly has always been a systematic theologian with a difference. He is also a poet and an occasional painter – not unlike St Alphonsus Liguori, founder of the Redemptorists, the religious congregation to which Fr Kelly belongs. Alphonsus was a moral theologian, a popular preacher, a poet and a painter as well as a bishop and founder. In these meditations, Tony Kelly also shows a prismatic sensibility, offering reflections which are more than systematic theology conventionally understood.

Crucially too, they are meditations born not just of thought but of prayer. As the Passion Narrative moves to its climax, Pilate brings Jesus out to the crowd after scourging and before sentencing. 'Behold the man', he says; and beholding is very much part of the Holy Week experience. We are urged to see Jesus, above all on the Cross, with the contemplative eye which understands what it sees. The disciples did not understand what they had seen. The two on the road to Emmaus say to the stranger who walks with them, 'Our hope had been that he would be the one to set Israel free' (Lk 24:21). They had seen Jesus die on the Cross, but they had thought this was the collapse of all hope, the end; and so they walk away from the city of death. Only once their eyes are opened in the encounter with the Risen Christ are they able finally to see what the Cross means; and then they return to Jerusalem through the night, not because the city is different but because they see with different eyes. In these meditations Tony Kelly turns to the events of Holy Week with a theologian's mind but with a contemplative eye which takes us further. It is the contemplative eye that enables us to move from astonishment into the ecstasy of which Fr Kelly speaks in these texts. He says that joy is the goal of the journey of Holy Week; and with that joy comes the ecstasy of Easter which Christianity has associated with the Holy Spirit.

But neither the joy nor the ecstasy of Easter comes too quickly. As Tony Kelly notes, we cannot 'rush to the resurrection'. Good Friday has to be bad Friday before it can be Good; Holy Saturday has to be unholy Saturday before it can be Holy. That is why these meditations, like Holy Week itself, take us slowly into deep and dark places. They descend even into hell, 'that point of God-forsakenness', Fr Kelly writes, "where hope is most tempted to despair . . . the regions of ultimate dread, the point most distant from God . . . where darkness reigns, words run out, and death is at its deadliest.'

They have at their heart a contemplation of the Cross. In pondering the Cross, Tony Kelly turns first to the earliest voice in the New Testament, the Apostle Paul, focusing chiefly on the Corinthian letters. Echoing Paul, Fr Kelly stresses the shock and scandal of the Cross, which overturns all the wisdom of this world, to the point of seeming madness. Having to proclaim the Crucified Christ in the Hellenistic world, he notes, made Paul 'naked and vulnerable'. Among the sophisticates of Athens Paul makes no mention of the crucifixion though they find his mention of the resurrection ludicrous enough (Acts 17:32). Coming to Athens, the intellectual, spiritual and artistic capital of the Greco-Roman world, must have been a highpoint in Paul's mission. His hopes would have been high as he mounted the Areopagus with the Parthenon looming above him. Yet there is no evidence that his mission in Athens was successful, since success for Paul meant the establishment and survival of a Christian community; and there is no sign of that in Athens. At least we have no letter of Paul to the Athenians. Athens, then, may well have been a failure for Paul, and the question is why. In his speech on the Areopagus (Acts 17:16–34), Paul mentions many things, all of them good and true, but the one thing he does not mention is the Cross, which would have been a bridge too far for the Athenians; and that may be why his mission failed in Athens. He then retreats south to Corinth where he comes to a new and deeper sense of the centrality of the Cross; and out of this sense he writes what we find in 1 Corinthians 1–2, 'We preach Christ crucified', and only him.

For Paul, the truth of the Cross was confirmed by his own experience of the apostolic mission, which I presume is true also of Tony Kelly. Time and again, efforts were made to silence or stop Paul. He was persecuted, punished and imprisoned; but what he came to see was that all these efforts to silence or stop him only gave his mission greater impetus. He writes the Letter to the Philippians from prison, saying that his imprisonment 'has served to advance the Gospel' (1:12). It has had the opposite effect to the one intended. The final attempt to silence and stop Paul for good was his execution in Rome on the road to Ostia. It happened at a place now called *Tre Fontane* (Three Fountains) because the ultimate wounds of beheading became a three-fold fountain springing up all around the world. His martyrdom ensured that Paul's voice would be heard till the end of time and into eternity, the voice of him who said, 'when I am weak, then I am strong' (2 Cor 12:10), the voice of the Crucified.

Paul is a decisive voice for Tony Kelly in seeking to understand what we see. But so too is John whose account we hear on Good Friday. Here we find the horror of crucifixion as precisely the place where the divine glory is revealed. That is the shock. John tells the atrocious story of Jesus' passion and death, yet his figure of Jesus has a majesty about it. Fr Kelly makes much of the shocking difference between divine glory and human glory.

It was the clash between the two which led to the Fall (Gen 3:1–7). The catechesis of evil on the lips of the serpent sets God's glory over and against human glory. According to the serpent, the two are locked in mortal combat: it is one or the other. Beyond the Fall, divine and human glory have to be brought into harmony, God's glory redounding to ours and vice versa. That harmony comes only in a perfectly obedient Jesus on the Cross. That is why the Philippians hymn has Jesus descending into hell in his 'death on a Cross' (2:8). But from that depth he is raised by the Father to glory, with 'every tongue confessing that Jesus Christ is Lord to the glory of God the Father' (2:11). It is not divine glory at war with human glory: it is the two together in perfect harmony. That is the story of John's Passion, and it is the story that Tony Kelly tells here.

These meditations stress the irony that pervades Holy Week and indeed the entire Bible. Nothing is what it seems to be. Irony depends on and feeds off a two-tiered view of reality – what seems to be and what is. To understand what we see in Holy Week is to move from the world of what seems to be into the world of what is. Jesus' death seems like the end but it is the beginning; what seems like death is birth; what seems like defeat is victory. Pilate sets over Jesus' head what seems to be a statement of his supposed crime, 'Jesus of Nazareth King of the Jews', but which is in fact a proclamation of the truth. Tony

Kelly is a good guide as we journey with him through Holy Week out of the world of what seems to be, the world of illusion, into the world of what is, the world of truth. Only in making that journey can we proclaim rather than lament the death of Jesus. That journey leads us beyond 'looking on the one whom they have pierced' (Zech 12:10). Fr Kelly makes it clear that we do not just look on the one pierced: we are drawn into Christ's sacrifice, into his way of seeing and being in the world, into his imagination, which makes possible a new humanity.

These meditations show the author to be a sensitive reader of the New Testament texts, with a sharp eye for detail which is always important in reading the Bible. But he is also adept at addressing larger themes in a way more typical of a systematic theologian. For instance, there are some telling reflections here on the cosmic dimension of the events of Holy Week. The entire universe is drawn into the Easter triumph of Jesus: 'in him the whole of creation awakes to find itself to be heaven-in-the-making'; and this has implications for what successive popes have called our 'ecological conversion'.

Perhaps the most original and theologically the most profound of the meditations is the one on the Ascension, which both does and does not take us beyond Holy Week. Tony Kelly claims that 'the whole meaning of the New Testament is found within the Ascension', which does not take Jesus out of time 'but is the condition for his complete immersion in it, as its fulness'. Far from being some kind of excarnation, Fr Kelly says, the Ascension is 'the completion and expansion of the incarnation'. He goes on to make some illuminating remarks on the connection between the Ascension of Jesus and the Assumption of Mary. This is a meditation which will repay much reading and reflection.

In founding the Congregation of the Most Holy Redeemer, St Alphonsus gave the new community as a motto the words of Psalm 130, *Copiosa apud eum redemptio*, 'In him there is abundant redemption'. An abundance of divine redemption is found in Jesus Christ, and an abundance of human and spiritual creativity was found in St Alphonsus. The same has been true of Tony Kelly, son of Alphonsus as he is; and these pages testify to that.

At times that line of the Psalm is translated 'In him is the fulness of redemption'; and there is a certain fulness in these meditations. They are late-life reflections from a man whose physical energies are not what they were but whose intellectual and spiritual energies remain intact. These meditations are the work of a man who, in seeking to make sense of his own diminishment, turns to Holy Week and finds his way into wonder. In these pages we find not only human and spiritual richness but also a theological maturity which has arrived at a simplicity focusing on what really matters. Holy Week, the Paschal Mystery, is where all Christian theology begins and ends. In that sense Christian theology is always essentially kerygmatic, as are these meditations. They are the work of a simplicity achieved.

What holds Fr Tony Kelly's many gifts and achievements together and makes them possible is a rare depth of humanity. Perhaps the first thing those who know him well would say of him is that Tony is a human being—one in whom we see the humanising and civilising power of the Gospel. The Gospel, like these meditations, focuses supremely on the death and resurrection of Jesus; and in the end it is not just Tony Kelly we meet in these pages but the crucified and risen Christ, whom we see and hear in all his wonderful strangeness. That makes these meditations not just a work of theology or textual interpretation or even spiritual attention, but a form of evangelical witness. Pope Paul VI noted that 'people today listen more to witnesses than to teachers, and if they listen to teachers it is because they are witnesses' (*Evangelii Nuntiandi,* 41). Here we find the mature reflections of one who has long been both teacher and witness.

Archbishop Mark Coleridge
Brisbane
November 2023

St Paul and the Cross

The first two chapters of St Paul's letter to the Corinthians are the classic introduction to the scandal of the Cross. There is a lively sense on the part of the apostle of the shocking uniqueness of the Christian message in this regard. Proclaiming Christ crucified was indeed a scandal to the culture of the day, and, indeed, to any philosophical or religious worldview. Shock and outrage resulted when Christian preaching of the Cross collided with settled religious convictions about the nature of the divine and how God was supposed to act. It was outrageous, therefore, to suggest that the supreme being had acted in such a weak an insane manner—so as to be revealed in this crucified Jesus. That was in stark contrast to everything what wisdom of the world had taken for granted.

Christian preaching of the Cross, however, made clear the extent to which he world's wisdom had been led astray. Preachers dared to state that a dreadful degradation of human nature had occurred when it condemned and put to death the Son of God. The implication was unavoidable: for whatever reason, God had chosen to be revealed to the world of political power and religious sensibilities through what had to be deemed extreme foolishness and weakness. Paul writes with a keen sense of paradox. If God's saving power was manifested in Christ crucified, it inevitably contradicted human expectations. Indeed, Paul's letter to the Corinthians, however paradoxical his message, exhibits an intense pastoral engagement and disappointment with a community that has become fragmented into cliques and partisan followings. Only a renewed sense of the folly of the Cross could instill into the conflict-ridden Corinthians a basic Christian common sense.

The Apostle's hope, as he clearly realised, was a little unrealistic in assuming 'that all of you will be in agreement and that there be no divisions among you, but that you be united in the same mind and same purpose' (1 Cor 1:10). He had heard from 'Chloe's people' that quarrels had broken out arising from rival allegiances, either to Paul or to Apollos, or to Cephas, or to Christ himself. In this overheated and competitive situation, Paul is forced to ask, 'Has Christ been divided? Or were you baptized in the name of Paul?' (1 Cor 1:10–13).

Such divisions and partisan allegiances can find their remedy only in the shock of the Cross and the paradoxical wisdom deriving from it—the revelation of God in the crucified Jesus. As a result, any attempt to appreciate the positive significance of the Cross had to appear foolishness to those locked in their own versions of wisdom. An arrogant sense of cultural superiority and self-sufficiency was indeed a mark characteristic of those 'who are perishing' (v 14). In contrast to the illusion of self-sufficiency, the Cross of Jesus comes as the revelation of God's saving power—however paradoxical—in those receptive to what the true God is doing. The pretentiousness of human wisdom ends in its repudiation as, in the words of the prophet, 'I will destroy the wisdom of the wise . . .' (Isa 29:14).

The Apostle had been sent to proclaim the gospel (v 17) in all its piercing, disconcerting truth. As a result, he could not but feel a certain nakedness and vulnerability. He is a burdened with the commission to preach what had occurred in Christ crucified. He had to make some kind of sense of what, religiously, philosophically and culturally, defied all sense. Paul's gospel of salvation was to be proclaimed in such 'unwise' terms. The Cross was repulsive to human sensibilities and subversive to assured human power and authority. It would mean that the Apostle had to defy the 'eloquent wisdom' of his day: There was a humiliating scandal in proclaiming God acting through the Cross of Jesus: 'For the message about the Cross is foolishness to those who are perishing, but to us who are being saved, it is the power of God' (v 18).

Paul's dismayed hearers, however, might appeal to venerable philosophical traditions and to conventional religious convictions to arm themselves against this new madness. Besides, the wisdom of the past inspired loyal citizens of the empire—who were unlikely to be impressed by an executed criminal. The Pauline preaching of the Cross challenged received notions of what constituted the good life for the decent citizen, to say nothing of what was entailed in seeking the supreme Good. In a particular manner, Paul's preaching of Christ crucified was a dissident, and a revolutionary point of view. It confronted the wisdom of past ages and the cherished attainments of the culture.

What Paul preached was, indeed, a profoundly shocking reality. He felt confident enough, however, to taunt the cultural authorities of his time: 'Where is the one who is wise? Where is the scribe? Where is the debater of this age?' (1 Cor 1:20). Scholars would surely retort that this particular Jewish dissident, this Paul, was laughably eccentric, and that he did not value the culture and wisdom even of his own people, to say nothing of that of the larger world. But Paul's conviction was clear: because God was to be proclaimed in the shocking guise of the Cross, with all its connotation of vulnerability and humiliation. In contrast, the accepted wisdom of the world was made to look ignorant and deluded.

Could the revelation of God be so linked to what that world most despises? There is a dreadful implication: God has acted only in this way of self-emptying and humility. The crucified Jesus belonged with those most shamed and despised in the world, with those so humbled and abased as to be left with no justification except what could come from God. The history of humanity's search in all its philosophies and religions is confronted with a terrible question: who is *this* God who is so out of harmony with the cherished ways of the world?

Paul drives home his conclusion: '. . . since, in the wisdom of God, the world did not know God through wisdom, God decided through the foolishness of our proclamation, to save those who believe' (1 Cor 1:21). Searchers for God must find the All-Holy One, present and acting in humiliation, weakness and in solidarity with the most despised of the world. It would take generations of faith for the Cross to be fully recognized as the signature of the divine. Habitual expectations of the world are found to be facing in the wrong direction. The conventional wisdom of the world was ill-prepared for the subversive way in which God would be revealed: For 'the Jews demand signs'. This accorded with their tradition and the sacred writings of the Torah, celebrated and expounded in Temple and synagogue. To them, God had been manifested as the mighty power to save, as the deliverer of the chosen people from slavery, exile and oppression. The whole trajectory of their tradition made the Jewish people seek out signs of God's continuing saving intention for his people, and of how the divine promise of salvation would be fulfilled.

For their part, 'the Greeks desire wisdom'. This was in accord with the classic philosophical tradition of searching for enlightenment. The educated mind was capable of grasping truth, and the ultimate reality behind it. In contrast, 'we proclaim Christ crucified, a stumbling block to the Jews and foolishness to the Gentiles' (v 23). Whatever the assurance of religion and the attainments of culture, Paul insists that, in Christ crucified the power and wisdom of God (v 24) are revealed. The shock to human sensibilities, both religious and philosophical, is exacerbated. The manner of God's saving action in the Cross catches everyone off-guard. It demands a new humility in the face of the incalculable ways of God. 'For God's foolishness is wiser than human wisdom and God's weakness if stronger than human strength' (1 Cor 1:25). The God of the Cross leaves all pretensions to human wisdom humbled, and confounds any self-confident reliance on power.

As Paul drives home his message, the Corinthian community is doubly confounded. Not only because it shares the common human condition, but also because this particular community, in Paul's estimation, does not, measure up to the highest standards of that humanity, however pretentious that might be:

> Consider your own call, brothers and sisters, not many of you were wise by human standards, not many were powerful, not many of noble birth (1 Cor 1: 26).

This is the cruelest cut: the saving power of God in Christ appears not only in weakness and apparent foolishness, but also seems to reserve a special place for the weakness and lowly status of the Corinthians themselves:

> But God chose what is foolish in the world to shame the wise; God chose what is weak in the world to shame the strong; God chose what is low and despised in the world, things that are not, to reduce to nothing things that are, so that no one might boast in the presence of God (1 Cor 1:27–29).

An intriguing question hangs in the air. Has Paul's conviction concerning the folly of the Cross and the weakness that it signifies been too successful? Did he in fact open the way to a kind of defeatism, and even self-hatred for that early Christian community? Little wonder that a remarkable development in Christian consciousness occurred when confronted by the shock of the Cross. Far from intensifying a mood of misery and defeat, there is was a glory that is revealed even greater than the glory of God's revelation to Israel. The ministry of Paul is not to be understood as a ministry of misery, ending in the glorification of suffering and degradation. In contrast, the Apostle remains always an agent of true glory as it is to be discovered on the face of Christ. Though Paul's appearance and rhetorical abilities may have been dismissed as of no account, his conviction of the dignity of his ministry of reconciliation never loses its confidence. The boldness (*parrhesia*) in his proclamation of the reality of God's saving will disclosed through the Cross is absolute.

According to Paul, the divine promise of salvation, for both the Corinthians and the rest of humankind, leaves them lacking the ability and even without the disposition to receive it. There can be no self-salvation; nor any room for self-congratulation on the part of any human being. The only assurance is to be found in the Cross of Christ:

> He is the source of your life in Christ Jesus who became for us wisdom from God, and righteousness and sanctification and redemption, in order that, as it is written, Let the one who boasts, boast in the Lord (1 Cor 1:31).

God has given to believers the all-sufficiency of Christ. He embodies true wisdom, and sets lowly humanity on the path to true freedom. Yet in addressing his Corinthians, Paul has eschewed any attempt to communicate the mystery of God through the techniques of rhetoric or wisdom. Although his communication is in fact marked by an extraordinary subtle and skillful rhetoric, his concentration is on the Cross as the shocking mode of God's self-revelation. His aim is not to offer his readers a highly wrought new theory, let alone charm them with rhetorical techniques. His intention is to expose his hearers/readers more deeply and immediately to the truth of the crucified Christ. High sounding words of spiritual or philosophical wisdom had to yield to an intense concentration on the reality of the Cross. That meant for Paul that he had to decide to 'know nothing among you except Jesus Christ, and him crucified' (1 Cor 2:2–3). Consequently, he freely admits that he had come to his apostolic task with a feeling of weakness and vulnerability: after all, his message was bewildering to his own people and derided by the cultural leaders of his day: 'I came to you in weakness and in fear and in much trembling' (1 Cor 2:4). That feeling of weakness and vulnerability prevented him from relying on any authority or influence he might have in terms of his own skills or abilities. He was forced therefore to act in accord the content of his message, with the word of the Cross, in a way that presupposed nothing but what God was communicating in Christ crucified. Consequently, he had to adopt the style of communication attuned to what he preached and dependent on its power:

> My speech and my proclamation were not with plausible words of wisdom, but with a demonstration of the Spirit and with power, so that your faith might rest not on human wisdom but on the power of God (1 Cor 4:5).

Not only was the content of his message to be centred on the scandal of the Cross, but also that the style of his communication must owe nothing to the arrogance of human skill or its powers of persuasion. Despite his protestations, Paul does in fact hope for a hearing among the 'mature' who are capable of discerning the wisdom that only God can give. The crucial particularity of Christ contrasts with the universal philosophies and wisdom found in the past. In consequence, the Pauline wisdom of the Cross cannot but be radically and dramatically countercultural in its impact. A collision with prevailing cultural and religious assumptions was inevitable: the elites who effectively presided over the institutions of culture and power were outraged. For Paul, all forms of self-promotion are contrary to true wisdom of the Cross, and destined to move in ever-tighter circles of self-destruction. The obsessions of human power or glory were doomed to perish in the rivalries and conflicts inherent in their self-serving frames of reference. On the other hand, there is another wisdom at work: 'Yet among the mature we do speak wisdom, though it is not a wisdom of this age or of the rulers of this age, who are doomed to perish' (1 Cor 2:6).

In the mind of Paul and in the minds of 'the mature', there is evidence of God's wisdom, working unpretentiously and all-but anonymously through the whole course of human history from its very beginning: 'But we speak God's wisdom, secret and hidden, which God decreed before he ages, for our glory' (1 Cor 2:7). This exceptionally paradoxical wisdom is found in Christ remains, who remains the one whom the builders rejected. Despite the darkness of rejection, the Cross shines a light into the gloom of a sinful world, and unmasks the foolish pretensions of human power and calculation 'None of the rulers of this age understood this: for if they had, they would not have crucified the Lord of glory' (1 Cor 2:8).

Paul goes on to appeal to the prophecy of Isaiah to provide a context for the hidden mystery at work: 'But, as it is written, "what no eye has seen, nor ear heard, nor the human heart conceived, what God has prepared for those who love him" [Isa 64:4]' (1 Cor 2: 9). The wisdom of the Cross can be revealed only through the witness of the Spirit. The hidden wisdom of God can never be reduced to the calculations and comprehension of human wisdom in its sciences and philosophies: 'These things God has revealed to us through the Spirit' (1 Cor 2:10). The wisdom of the Cross is not only to hidden to human comprehension, but resides in the innermost spirit God, 'for the Spirit searches everything, even the depths of God' (1 Cor 2:11). Paul here proceeds to employ a human analogy based on the experience of inwardness and interiority. What is truly 'within' the mind and heart is disclosed only through the deep personal awareness and self-presence. It is disclosed in acts of understanding and moral responsibility. There lies the basis of personal identity, the deepest experience of what and who we are: 'For what human being knows what is truly human except the human spirit that is within? So also no one comprehends what is truly God's except the Spirit of God' (1 Cor 2:12). Only through the testimony of God's inmost Spirit can believers come to recognise the divine wisdom displayed in the Cross. That divine Spirit brings a new capacity to penetrate and assimilate the wisdom of the Cross—for oneself and all prospective believers:

> Now we have received not the spirit of the world, but the Spirit that is from God, so that we may understand the gifts bestowed on us by God. And we speak of these things in words not taught by human wisdom, but taught by the Spirit, interpreting spiritual things to those who are spiritual (1 Cor 2: 12–13).

The wisdom of the Cross, therefore, is not an attainment of human intelligence but a communication from the inmost consciousness of

God. Only God's Spirit reveals to human beings the saving purpose God in the Cross, despite its mundane, eccentric appearance as foolishness and weakness. Without the illumination of the Spirit, without a certain 'connaturality' and attunement to the Spirit, the Cross remains impenetrable and resistant to human intelligence:

> Those who are unspiritual do not receive the gifts of God's Spirit, for they are foolishness to them, and they are unable to understand them, because they are spiritually discerned. Those who are spiritual discern all things, and they are subject to no one else's scrutiny (1 Cor 2:14–15).

Paul concludes that only the Spirit of God can inspire the cruciform wisdom of God. By implication, only those receptive to the word of the Cross receive the gift of understanding it, along with the strength to withstand the contradiction of a world that sees its salvation elsewhere. Moreover, Paul confidently asserts that attunement to the Cross is itself a manifestation of the mind of Christ: 'For who has known the mind of the Lord, so as to instruct him?' (Isa 40:13). But we have the mind of Christ (1 Cor 2:16). Through the witness of the Spirit, believers receive the gift of a new wisdom that brings both conformity to the mind of God and participation in the consciousness of the crucified Christ himself.

A larger context

In the ancient world the Cross was an obscene reality. It was a mode of execution reserved to slaves and subverters of the empire, designed to deter any threat to the *Pax Romana*, the imperial peace. Only when crucifixion as a form of execution had been abolished by Constantine three hundred years later would the Cross became a Christian symbol. Many today who gladly wear a Cross as an emblem of Christian commitment can hardly imagine the degree emotional revulsion associated with connecting divine revelation to such a hideous form of death, crucifixion. That God could be revealed in this crucified victim had to be experienced as religious scandal and a philosophical folly—'a stumbling block to the Jews and foolishness to the Gentiles' (1 Cor 1:23). In other words, the Cross of Christ was the most radical form of culture shock. Surely God could not be, would not act, like *that*!—disclosed to the world as a criminal tried and executed by imperial Rome.

Yet precisely at this point of utter dismay and revulsion, the sheer excess of divine mercy and compassion was displayed. In the Cross of Jesus the excess of our human capacity for evil was outwitted by that excess of love on God's part which 'not anything in all creation' (Rom 8:39) could counter. In the providence of love working in and through all events of our history, the most demonic gesture of human evil comes to dramatise the ecstatic extravagance of God's mercy on sinful humanity: 'Christ died for the ungodly . . . God proves his love for us in that while we were yet sinners Christ died for us' (Rom 5:6–11).

The love of Christ goes to an unimaginable limit. It reaches that point human history is found to be most against God, and most enclosed in the vicious circle of violence and despair. Yet hope stirred—for a new humanity in defiance of the power of death and all evil, suffered or inflicted. Here was the divine breakthrough into the world at the furthermost limit of its alienation from God: 'to those who are called, both Jews and Greeks, Christ the power of God and the wisdom of God' (1 Cor 1:24).

The impossible possibilities of divine love are manifested in this most innocent of the world's victim. Let the powers of this world do as they will, let evil display its most demonic intensity, this truth will stand. For here was 'God's wisdom, secret and hidden, which God decreed before the ages for our glory' (1 Cor 2:7). So surprisingly hidden is the wisdom of love concealed in this crucified man that 'none of the rulers of this age understood this; for if they had they would not have crucified the Lord of glory' (v 8). The power of evil must hide from itself its own destructiveness—and its own defeat. Unable to imagine any reality beyond itself, it is imprisoned in its own desperate futility. But there is another imagination born of divine compassion: 'to those who are called, both Jews and Greeks, Christ the power of God and the wisdom of God' (1 Cor 1:24). God appears in q new guise. The Father to whom Jesus prays is revealed as the engendering original love that refuses any presence to the world except as the one who gives and glorifies his crucified Son. In his turn, the Son rejects any identity amongst us save as the one who is totally surrendered to his Father's saving love for all. In this revelation of the One God, the Spirit will act only as that power of self-giving love whereby the Father gives his Son, and the Son surrenders all to the Father for our salvation.

In the decades that followed this event, the first generation of Christians had their own experience of weakness and persecution.

They lovingly contemplated the Cross as the disclosure of the wisdom of God. By unmasking the human capacities to destroy and deface our true selves, the Cross stood for a great reversal and a new beginning. God would not add evil to evil by wreaking divine vengeance on sinful humanity. For, through the Cross, a greater good would use this evil for its own loving purpose; and a way would be opened to turn the sin-enclosed world to God.

The glory that Paul will speak of in his second letter to the Corinthians is a glory that continues to be a scandal to all worldly pretensions and cultural criteria. The Son's inglorious departure from this world through condemnation and crucifixion is acknowledged as a glory of another kind. It is obviously not the glory of human success and the human achievement. Nor, as Paul has already pointed out, is it the glory of human reputation and fame. Rather, it is a particular glory communicated in what we have been calling 'the shock of the Cross' and the transformation of human sensibilities and perception of values that this will entail.

....

Jesus knew our evils. The Word had truly become flesh and dwelt among us. As a mortal man he suffered death, to be swallowed up into the silence, darkness, poverty, powerlessness and separation that mark all our dying. In his death there are the further intensities of suffering: agony of mind and body, betrayal, abandonment, condemnation, torture, mockery, failure, execution . . . He suffers death as one put to death, when everything is wrapped in the greatest darkness of all, the sense of the terrifying absence of God in an impenetrably God-forsaken world.

The Cross is the climax of the power of darkness. God appears as banished from his good creation, just as that creation appears shut in its own malice and hopelessness. In condemning the Son to the Cross, the injustice of the world appears as just; and the crucified Son, far from being accepted as the bringer of the Kingdom and the true form of our humanity, appears as a criminal. He is 'counted among the wicked' (Mk 15, 28), 'made sin' (2 Cor 5:21). He 'has become a curse for us, for it is written 'Cursed by everyone who hangs on a tree' (Gal 3:13).

The reality of his Cross is the focus of all the enigmatic experiences that make up the 'problem of evil': the defencelessness of the good, the absence of God, the immorality of 'morality', the human perversity of preferring to cause death rather than allow for life... The Cross stands as the sign of a world disowning its own grace and promise. It wrings from the crucified an agonised prayer, '*Eloi, Eloi, lama sabacthani*? My God, My God why hast thou abandoned me?', and culminates in his loud last cry as he breathes his last (Mk 15:34, 37).

Other Gospel accounts present the Cross as the highpoint of the freedom of Jesus, as he makes his ultimate surrender: 'Father, into your hands I commend my spirit' (Lk 23:46), and 'It is finished' (Jn 19:30). He yields himself into an incalculable mystery of God that God's grace may the more abound—even at this most impenetrable point of the world's darkness. Those who meditate on the passion of Christ are drawn into the drama of his naked self-surrender for the Cross discloses for believers the ultimate, the final reality of God. By killing Jesus it is as though power of evil challenges the mystery of God to reveal itself. It defies God to be truly God. God would not be God if love were defeated here. And God would have been defeated if the Father of mercies were to be finally reduced to the level of worldly powerplay, by answering evil with evil, and so making 'an eye for an eye and a tooth for a tooth' a cosmic law binding even the Father himself.

Yet there is no divine vengeance. The will of God is not changed into violence or revenge. The Father of Jesus is no mere worldly power. He sends no legion of angels. He who is turned to sinners in mercy refuses to have any presence in the world save that of the crucified Son. And as this Son prays for the forgiveness of those who have crucified him, he rejects any worldly identity, any worldly justification or protection save what the Father can be for him. At the point of demonic concentration of evil, he surrenders himself to an all-Holy Spirit as the last breath of his life. This Spirit, inspiring the selfgiving death of Christ for the many, has no other identity, works in no other power, than that of unconditional love. The trinitarian communion of selfsacrificing love brings a new crucified humanity into existence.

The scriptures represent in various ways the emergence of a new community gathered around the crucified Christ: Simon of Cyrene, the courageous presence of the faithful women, the 'the Good Thief' making his last prayer, Mary and the beloved disciple at the foot of the Cross, the Roman centurion declaring Jesus to be innocent, Joseph of Arimathea asking Pilate for the body...

By dying on the Cross, the man of parables becomes the supreme parable, of how God undoes the evil of the world, and forms our humanity anew. In an intensely personal moment, Paul can say, 'I live by the faithfulness of the Son of God who loved me and gave himself for me' (Gal 2:20).

These two Pauline letters, despite the remedial character of the second letter after what appears to have been a serious breakdown in communication between Paul and the Corinthians. Perhaps this failure was occasioned by the brutal starkness of Paul's 'word of the Cross'. It had undermined any religious or cultural smugness in the Corinthian community. It had to develop a more rounded Christian experience as it continued to delve into the basic phenomenology of the life of faith in the light of the Cross. The Cross of Jesus was not to be morbidly depressive as if to privilege defeatism and failure, just as it did not exclude all noble aspirations toward the true and the good (Phil 4:8–9). Paul will insist that it that the Cross communicates its own glory, but not in the human sense of bolstering pride in the achievements on which human reputations are built. As with the Johannine writings, despite the shock, humiliation and apparent failure, another glory is at work which reaches deep into Christian experience and imagination. This is not the glorification of defeat and misery, but the distinctive glory of God manifesting itself in a revelation and self-giving beyond anything the world could have imagined. The powers of darkness go into a final spasm, in seeking to repress the common conscience of what so fundamentally disturbs it. In the midst of this darkness, a love not of this world continues to come on its own terms. It works only in the power of what it is, revealed as a love that keeps on being love no matter what the rejection it suffers.

Jesus Washes the Disciples Feet

The explicit story of the Passion of the Lord rightly begins on Holy Thursday. On the evening of this day, the meal that Christian devotion has traditionally called 'the Last Supper' was held. It leads later that night to the 'Agony in the Garden' and to the arrest, imprisonment and cross-examination of Jesus which follow. After this meal, in what will happen later this night and on the morrow which will be his final day, Jesus will speak little, and even do little. He will borne along by the events that overtake him and send him to his death.

But in this final meal with his those who had stayed with him to this point, he will speak and act. In gesture and word, he will express the whole mission of his life and his deepest consciousness of what has been going on and of what is about to take place. He draws those with him into the deepest desires of his heart and shares with them his way of imagining the world far otherwise than those who were about to imprison, condemn, torture and execute him.

In the months and years to come, the disciples, who were with him at table in these hours as the darkness of that night thickened about them, will treasure memories of this final meal. And in the light of the great change that would affect all followed him, the earliest believers would remember his words, 'Do this is memory of me'.

He whose memory they celebrated had lived so differently. His every breath was a protest against the envy and violence which had given death its power to chill the human heart and to hide our world in its shadow. In our fear and despair and suspicion of God we human beings have all been complicit in the reign of death and dwelt in the shadow of death. But his life was different. 'The God of the living', the Father from whom he came, whose reign he proclaimed, whom we had loved with all his heart and with all his soul, with all his mind and with all his strength, was the wondrously merciful space in which life would be revealed in its deepest meaning. God was the ever-present and final reality, the life-giver judging and overturning all the petty idols enclosing us fear and isolation, and inviting us into something more which could never be fully expressed or possessed—unless by living 'in memory of him . . .'

To live in memory of him had its own special implications and demands. To imagine the world as he imagined it, to feel for the world as he felt for it, to change the world as he sought to change it, meant to know and serve God in a new way. It would demand an unreserved surrender to the God who inspired the imagination of Jesus, whose love filled his heart, whose saving will was at work in all his words and deeds.

The Gospels speak of a kind of divine necessity regarding the Cross that awaited him on the following day: 'The Son of Man must suffer many things . . . and be rejected . . . and be killed' (Mk 8:31; Mt 16:21; Lk 17:25). We human beings defend to the death the hard the little world we have made in our image. Anyone who bent on changing our death-bound world would be made to suffer and to face the power of death in all its ferocity. Any one so disturbing the peace would have to be prepared to pay the price; to be sacrificed, expelled, to be violently removed from the scene where other powers were jealously in control. So Jesus is not really the victim of a blind fate. His fate was all too predictable, given the violence of a history notoriously inhospitable to its prophets. Nor is he the victim of capricious divine will only to be satisfied with such a death. He was not disarming God by offering himself as a sacrifice. On the contrary, the true God, acting in his life and death of his Son, was working to disarm us. Through Jesus' suffering on our behalf, God revealed the murderous violence infesting our societies, and offered another possibility. What Jesus would undergo was the outcome of his passionate commitment to our real peace and to the humanity that God means us to share. In this respect, the clouds gathered about him, not over him from an angry heaven, but around him from a God-resistant humanity. For his solidarity with the poor and the lost, those excluded from the human table, brought its own consequences.

The old world content to use God for its purposes had no room for his version of God intent on making the world an open heaven, in which those content to live with God could breathe the free air of

God's own Spirit of truth and holiness. A self-enclosed humanity did not welcome this kind of upset; its idols did not need this kind of troubling.

In the liturgy of Holy Thursday, the Church recalls two symbolic actions performed by Jesus on this last night: he washed the disciples' feet; and he gave himself to them as their food and drink in the bread and wine of the eucharist.

> Now before the festival of the Passover, Jesus knew that his hour had come to depart from this world and go to the Father. Having loved his own who were in the world, he loved them to the end (Jn 13:1).

In the original Passover, Jesus recalled, along with all his fellow Jews, how God had delivered them from foreign captivity and formed a new people of God. The movement of what happened in that original event now reaches its moment of fulfilment. There would be a final liberation, an unsurpassable manifestation of God's saving love.

The decisive hour had come; all his life had looked to it; the times had run their course. The months through which Jesus proclaimed the salvation God was offering were now to reach their moment of truth. The world was to be opened to a new horizon of life. He was going from this world bounded by fear and death into that space of endless life and communion where his Father dwelt.

By leaving this world and going to God, he was not escaping to a divine realm indifferent to our human struggles. For his going to the Father was his way of remaining always with those he loved in a final life-giving way: 'unto the end'—not only to the end of his life, but to the fulfilment of all his loving relationship to them. By being totally turned to the Father, in that heart-to-heart relationship that had marked life (Jn 1:1, 18), he was to be turned toward his followers in the world in which they were at once left, and no longer at home. When he had gone, the home of their hearts had to be elsewhere: in the house of the Father where he was going to prepare a place for them (14:2). He was to be the way they now had to follow (14:6).

It was the hour when love had to prove itself in the presence of the forces of evil: 'The devil had already put it into the heart of Judas ... to betray him' (13:2). The outreach of love is here confronting the intimate presence of rejection and betrayal. But it is not frustrated.

In the course of that meal, when the heart of the Son was laid open to receive all that the Father had entrusted to him—'knowing that the Father had given all things into his hands' (v 3)—in the hour that was to disclose the truth of his identity and mission—'that he had come from God and was going to God'—he expressed all this in a bewildering gesture. He did not call his disciples to some further act of reverence; nor did he reproach them for their failures, their incomprehension and weakness. In an atmosphere loaded with the anticipation of some climactic revelation of God, the disciples watched in amazement. He got up from the table, took off his outer garment, draped a towel around him, and poured water into a dish; and then began to wash the disciple's feet and to dry them with the towel around him.

Peter protested. The Jesus whom this leader of the disciples had chosen to follow, to say nothing of the God he thought to serve, would surely be dishonoured if he, Peter, went along with this! But once more 'the Rock' (1:42) had to shaped to another reality. What counted was not Peter's view on how his master should act. Jesus called him to go beyond his set ideas on who God was and what God willed, into another world of truth: 'Unless I wash you, you have no share with me' (13:8). To be washed by the Lord was to be cleansed of the age-old encrustations which worked so effectively in keeping the true God at a distance. To be washed was to share in alternative sense of God, and in a deeper familiarity with Jesus himself. It meant, too, that Peter had to find himself anew, by awakening to a new sense of belonging to others and serving them. The way of the true God was the way of love; and the way of love makes those who follow it take the lowest place, the role of a servant, that others might be washed and nourished with the truth.

It was not only a matter of having one's feet washed by Jesus, as though everything was revealed when the disciple is humbled before the humble love of God. For this lowly, loving service of others had to continue. Jesus unfolds his gesture in the question, 'Do you know what I have done to you?' (v 12). In answering his own question that he had expressed in word and deed, he made it clear that we cannot use our religion to keep either God or our neighbour at a safe distance. We must allow ourselves to be drawn into the movement of divine life embodied in Jesus, to act as he has acted: 'So, if I, your Teacher and Lord, have washed your feet, you also ought to wash one another's feet' (v 14). We can no longer love God because we love no one. We cannot serve God without serving one another.

In this gesture, Jesus is not simply giving us good example, proposing an ideal or expressing a sublime idea, the better to inspire us to treat one another with sensitivity and respect. It is that; but it is more. We are not left looking at him as someone external to our lives, but invited to follow him in what was central to his life and its deepest movement: 'For I have set you a [supreme] example, that you also should do as I have done to you.' (v 15). The 'life to the full' (Jn 10:10) that Jesus offers has as its central feature and direction the humble service of others. By sharing in his self-giving we are to be made like him: 'Just as I have loved you, you also should love one another' (Jn 13:34). As a consequence, Christians can witness to the world. By being so taken out of ourselves, we form a new community of selfless love. Only when our witness is made effective in this way will our world, locked into its habitual forms of self-promotion and rivalry, be surprised by the grace of another possibility: 'By this will everyone know that you are my disciples' (v 35).

A further pointer to the meaning of this scene, at once so precious and so unsettling in Christian memory, is the teaching of St Paul when he invites the Philippians not 'to look to your own interests, but to the interests of others' (Phil 2:4). He goes on to summon them to imitate the self-giving character of Jesus: 'Let the same mind be in you that was in Christ Jesus' (v 5). The truth of the divine identity of Jesus was manifest in his unreserved service of others: 'though he was in the form of God . . . he emptied himself taking the form of a slave' (Phil 2:6–8). To believe in Christ is to 'Let the same mind' be in us, both in the community of the Church and in all our social interactions with our world.

The other-directed love of Christ is the basic momentum of all truly personal life, both as it is realised in God, and in humanity made in God's image. In Christian understanding, to be a person is to be for others. Most profoundly, by performing this gesture of washing his disciples' feet, Jesus is drawing us into the 'love-life' of the Trinity itself: 'Beloved, let us love one another, because love is from God; everyone who loves is born of God and knows God. Whoever does not love, does not know God, for God is love' (1 Jn 4:7–8).

The full meaning of Jesus' washing his disciples' feet will be disclosed on the Cross. It is celebrated in the Church in the sacrament of Baptism. In those waters, the Lord washed us clean and unites us to himself in his life of love. In the Church's liturgy, the mystery of love comes to its most intense expression in the Eucharist. Through this sacrament faith celebrates the gift Jesus made us of his body and blood in order to nourish us into a community of new and endless life.

The gift of God can never be fully described. The Son is incarnate as truly human and exposed to all human limitations. He knows the darkest of all human experiences—failure, abandonment and betrayal, condemnation, torture, execution, burial as a criminal.

Yet, to be 'for us' is the basic impetus of Jesus' life and mission. He lives to do God's saving will, and lays down his life for the lost, 'for the many', for 'the world'.

His divine character as Son of the Father makes him uniquely related to all.

His whole being is offered to nourish us, for whose sake he lived and died: 'This is my body given up for you, my blood poured out: do this in memory of me' (Matt 26:26–28).

Though John's Gospel does not contain a Eucharistic formula of institution like the other Gospels, it does lead its readers into a deep understanding of the Eucharist, especially in chapter 13. Jesus is focused on a decisive moment: 'when Jesus knew that his hour had come . . .' (Jn 13:1b). It is *his* hour, the climax toward which the Father's will had guided him. It is his hour because it is his Father's hour.

In it the whole course of human history will be condensed and fulfilled, for Jesus. As Son of the Father, is about to 'to pass out of this world to the Father' from whom he was sent (Jn 13:1b). In life, and now in the death he is about to die, Jesus has been moving toward the Father. Jesus has passed through a world of conflicts, divisions, rejection and terminal antagonism toward the true God.

His mission was intent on opening that world to the loving will/presence of the Father. In his return to the Father, God will be revealed to the world as its original lover and the ultimate end (Jn 3:16).

The more Jesus moves toward the Father, the more he manifests the Love that God is: 'having loved his own who were in the world, he loved them to the end' (Jn 13:1c). In going to the God who so loved the world as to give himself for the life of the world, the Son embodies the limitlessly self-giving extent of the Father's love.

By washing his disciples' feet, the Son reveals the true character of the Father. His gesture sums up all his words and deeds to this point, and anticipates the full meaning of the hour that has now arrived.

The Last Supper

The Love welling up from the Father, breathed, forth in the Spirit, and expressed in the Son confronts evil through the Cross.

In this confrontation, love is not defeated, diminished or changed into something else when it meets the full force of evil, its opposite and contradiction.

This love is unconditional despite the fact that Jesus, the Son of the Father, is rejected, condemned and executed.

The Love that he embodied kept on being love, 'to the end' (Jn 13:1b).

God's love is not changed into hatred or resentment. It outstrips all human limits and contradictions.

It outwits the wisdom of a world built on revenge and retaliation and self-defence. The light of Love, AND the darkness of evil (Jn 1:5), BUT the darkness does not overcome it. Through the Cross, the light of Love shines most brightly in the darkness of evil, hatred, violence and despair.

The truth of Love shows itself—and exposes the power of evil for what it is.

The excess of evil calls forth the greater excess of love—and mercy for evil doers In the mystery of the Cross, love claims even the dreaded realm of death to display its generosity, and the extreme to which it goes.

Love absorbs the menace of death into itself, not as an ending of life but as the permanent and unconditional character of living and giving.

Death no longer appears as a fearful barrier cutting us off from life, and the God of life and love but as entry into life of God.

Death now is revealed as the extreme to which God's love has gone so that the Cross becomes the revelation of divine compassion and mercy.

The Eucharist and the Last Supper

In Luke's Gospel, Jesus' last meal with his Disciples occurs in the context of his many meals with different types of people. To a striking degree, he was a most convivial man. For example, he was an honoured guest at a great banquet put on by Levi, the tax collector, who had left everything to follow him (Lk 5:27–32). Devout pharisees were critical of the way Jesus mixed with such company. But he reminded them that it was the sick who needed the doctor (Lk 5:31).

When eating with Simon, one of these Pharisees, a woman of ill-repute sought him out. To the astonishment of all, she bathed his feet with her tears, dried them with her hair, and began anointing them with precious ointment (Lk 7:36–50). When Simon was understandably shocked at such extravagant intimacy, Jesus contrasted the cool reception his host had given him with the love that the poor woman was showing. He then proceeded to declare her sins forgiven, praised her faith and sent her away in peace.

When Jesus had welcomed the big crowd that had followed him out into the countryside, and the twelve were beginning to wonder how they could be fed, he insisted that apostles share out their own scant provisions. And so he blessed and broke the five loaves and two fish, and fed the whole hungry gathering (Lk 9:12–17).

In the course of his travels, after Martha had welcomed him into her home, she complained that her sister Mary was too absorbed with listening to him and not helping with the work. He reminded his generous hostess that eating with him was a symbol of something far greater than merely sharing in an array of good dishes (Lk 10:38–42).

When another of the pharisees, having invited him home, expressed surprise that Jesus did not perform the ritual washing before the meal, he warned that purity of heart was the issue, not external display (Lk 11:37–41).

Dining with another eminent religious leader on a Sabbath day, he gave a lesson on what that holy day should mean. It was to be a time for healing, not for ignoring the sick (Lk 14:1–6); a time for humble solidarity with the lowly (vv 7–11), not for lording it over them (vv 12–14); a time for open-hearted generosity to all, not for the calculation of social advantage; a time of openness to the gifts of God, not for distraction by lesser concerns (vv 15–24).

Then, at his entry into the house of the Zachaeus, an exploitative tax gatherer, Jesus brought salvation with him. This hard man became a benefactor to the poor and a man of justice. One who had been lost had been sought out, and had been found (Lk 19:1–11).

A story of many meals. Afterward, too, when the days of grief and fear had passed, his followers could not but report his presence to them except in the setting of meals. When the disciples on the road to Emmaus pressed the mysterious stranger to stay with them, he did stay, and ate with them, so that they could tell the others how 'he had made himself known to them in the breaking of the bread' (Lk 24:13–35). Later, when he appeared to apostles and a larger gathering of disciples, he asked for food to prove he was still the one who had eaten with them, even if now present as the Risen Lord (Lk 24:36–43).

The Last Supper, then, was, in a sense, a meal to end all meals, for it summed up all that he had taught and done before, and all he would become in the lives of his followers afterwards.

In its celebration of the eucharist, the Church is forever carrying out his command to eat and drink in memory of him, to draw from him its deepest life and love. The liturgical words are familiar. After giving praise to the Father as the source of all gifts and invoking the transforming power of the Holy Spirit, the eucharistic prayer goes on:

> On the night he was betrayed, he took bread and gave you thanks and praise. He broke the bread, gave it to his disciples and said: 'Take this, all of you, and eat it: this is my body which will be given up for you.'
>
> When supper was ended, he took the cup. Again he gave you thanks and praise, gave the cup to his disciples and said: 'Take this all of you and drink from it: this is the cup of my blood, the blood of the new and everlasting covenant. It will be shed for you and for all, so that sins may be forgiven. Do this in memory of me.'

This is the 'the mystery of faith' to be proclaimed in our lives: 'Lord, by your Cross and resurrection, you have set us free. You are the Saviour of the world.'

By recalling his self-gift under the symbols of the bread and wine, we are summoned into the depths of his imagination and drawn into his passion to bring into existence a world transformed in God's saving love.

In his previous meals with the sinful and the outcast he had declared that it was the sick who needed the doctor. In the eucharist he gives himself to us sinners for our healing and forgiveness: 'my body given up for you' . . . 'my blood shed for you, and for all, that sins may be forgiven.'

Long ago, a sinful woman of the city had washed and dried his feet with her hair, and then anointed them with perfume. Through the eucharist, we are invited into an even deeper intimacy with him. He gives us himself to us as our food and drink, to nourish our experience of the forgiveness and peace that only God can give.

In an isolated spot, he had called on the disciples to share their meagre supplies with the crowd; and multiplied their resources in a wonderful way. Now, the bread and wine of our lives is transformed and multiplied by him to feed our hunger, and to sustain the life to the whole Church in all generations.

In the celebration of the eucharist, we too lay aside the busy preoccupations of Martha, and follow Mary, to receive from God the one necessary sustenance—Jesus himself, the source of the holy communion of all believers.

We too are drawn beyond the fixations on external ritual characteristic of the devout pharisees, to receive from him that food and drink which alone can transform us from within—'so that sins may be forgiven'.

The eucharist celebrates a new covenant as the culminating manifestation of the love and mercy of God. It would leave no room for proud ranking of ourselves above others, for we are united in receiving the sheer gift of God, love pouring itself out so that we might all be caught up in its outpouring—loving others as we have been loved.

In the eucharist, like Zachaeus, we are sought and found; and salvation comes to us in the love of Christ, the gift that brings all other gifts with it.

In 'the breaking of the bread', Jesus makes himself known to us at this later time. Nourished by this meal, we are drawn into his imagination; and. in doing what he commands us to do, it is we who form the world into a new hope and a new sense of God. Under all these aspects, he is still with us as the man of many meals, because, in that final gesture of love, he made himself food and drink for us in our journey of faith.

On that night, however, when the darkness was closing in, there would seem little hope of salvation. While he eats with his disciples, threat and condemnation are hanging in the air. Some great trial is impending. He would be abandoned to his fate. A sense of foreboding grew. Where was God now? Only God could save him, for no on else could . . . 'Before I suffer . . .' (Lk 22:15–21).

Yet, even on this night of betrayal and desertion on the part of his followers, he looks forward; beyond what is about to happen to him, out to what is to happen to them, and to all future generations of believers. His life even here is still a song of praise and thanksgiving, a dedication to the God who is acting in all the darkness that surrounds him, to the Father who is with the Son in a bond of unbreakable love: 'He took bread and gave you thanks and praise.'

The bread; his body; our food: 'take this and eat it, this is my body which will be given up for you.' It is the language of ultimate love, to be the food of those he loves. He will be given up, eaten up, handed over, to torture, condemnation, mockery, death. It is food for those who too will suffer with him in the cause of God. It is a gift that will never be exhausted. For love keeps of being love, ever impatient with the way things are, a gift coming to us in the most humble of all the elements of our daily nourishment, yet now transformed in a giving beyond any human expectation. It is the gift we most need, that only he can give, that only he is, given right into the depths of our hunger and weakness: 'I am the bread of life. Whoever comes to me will never by hungry . . .' (Jn 6:35). It is offered to us where we are most starved of love, when we are so isolated in our separate selves that no one love can reach or call us. To a world starving in its capacities to be one in love and justice, he gives us the body of another humanity: 'For the bread of God is that which comes down from heaven and gives life to the world' (Jn 6:33).

The wine; his blood; our drink: 'This is the cup of my blood.' The cup of wine he held in his hands symbolises that blood which will drip from his lacerated back during the scourging and run down his face after the thorns were pressed into his head, and flow to the ground as he hangs on the Cross; the blood of all his suffering, blood shed that we might live: 'my blood is true drink' (Jn 6:55).

Again, the ecstatic language of love: under the transforming power of the Spirit, in the eucharistic cup believers drink the blood of a love without limit, of a passion that spends itself for the salvation of the world, of a life poured out 'for you and for all'. It is the wine of God's excess, of the folly of divine mercy. The excess of love meets the excess of lovelessness, 'that sins may be forgiven'. This blood is not the blood of violence or divine vengeance. In this blood, an infinite love, refusing to be anything but itself, bleeds, wounded and ever vulnerable to a world that sheds the blood on the innocent. This blood is mixed with the blood of all martyrs for the truth. Yet Jesus is more than one more innocent victim. Because of him, the blood martyrs will not be shed in vain. There is love at work, greater than any power that evil can exert to murder and destroy: 'The blood of the new and everlasting covenant.' The blood that will be shed here has the power to bind the heart of God to the fate of our suffering humanity: 'Those who eat my flesh and drink my blood have eternal life, and I will raise them up on the last day; for my flesh is true food and my blood is true drink' (Jn 6:54-55).

Jesus and 'The Good Thief'

'Jesus, remember me when you come into your kingdom' (Lk 23:42). One of the dying criminals speaks to the dying Jesus in words which express one of the most intimate and touching prayers in all of the Gospels.

The criminal concerned has been known in popular devotion as 'the Good Thief'. Such a description is not quite accurate. After all, there is no reason to think of him as 'good', since he admits that he has been 'justly condemned, for we are getting what we deserve for our deeds' (v 41). Nor, most probably, was he a thief, since the Gospels speak of him as a 'wrongdoer' or a 'bandit'. But he does make a remarkable request. He does not address Jesus in the more customary formal terms—such as 'Lord' or 'Rabbi' or 'Son of David'–but simply as 'Jesus', in a directness unparalleled in the Gospels. Jesus, 'this man who has done nothing wrong' (v 41), is there with him to be called on—despite the wretched fate they both share.

His prayer is a marvellously ironic turn in the story of the passion. Jesus replies, 'Truly I tell you, today you will be with me in paradise' (v 43). Given the tragic drama being enacted, it is hardly possible to talk about the Gospel's sense of humour. But is it not an extraordinary form of black comedy when a criminal turns to a man being crucified with him to ask his fellow sufferer to remember him when he comes into his kingdom? The irony is all the more piercing when this Jesus assures his companion in torture and execution that on this very day they will be reunited in paradise? Did the ways of the world that had brought both of them to this desperate point matter so little? How could such a promise be made in the midst of such an unpromising situation?

Up to this point, the Gospel has been recounting what amounts to a crescendo of rejection directed against the man who makes this promise, this Jesus. Satan had entered into Judas, one of his chosen disciples, to inspire his betrayal. The chief priests and officers of the Temple police had moved to implement the plot to get rid of him. The disciples, even to the end, disputing about who was to be greater, are distinguished, in the event, only by the various manners in which they misunderstood and abandoned him. Peter, their leader, denies him three times. He is mocked by the guards in courtyard of the high priest, then taken to the formally condemned by the leaders of his own people; whereupon he is taken to Pilate. After the Roman official hears the accusations, he sends the accused to Herod where he meets with further contempt and mockery. On being delivered back to Pilate, Jesus hears the crowd calling for the release of Barabbas in his place. Pilate gives in, and the Cyrene is pressed into serve in carrying the Cross. The lamentation of grieving women accompanied his last journey through the city. On reaching Golgotha, he is nailed to the Cross in the company of two known criminals. One of the criminals derides him for his hopeless failure—and the other groans out a strange request.

But this prayer of the crucified criminal has been preceded by another prayer, that of the crucified Son: 'Father, forgive them, for they do not know what they are doing' (v 34]. The prayer of the innocent one to the all-merciful Father (Lk 6:36) who gives to those who ask, who brings home those who search, who opens the door to those who knock, who gives the Holy Spirit to those pray, is now answered. Grace is at work in the prayer of the crucified wrongdoer, in the very fact that he prays, and in the promise that Jesus gives. In the exchange between these two crucified men, the great mystery of all-merciful love is being disclosed.

Divine forgiveness begins to upset and change the world. As the darkness gathers, and the light of the sun itself is dimmed, as the veil of the temple is torn in two (vv 44–45), Jesus cries with a loud voice, 'Father, into your hands I commend my spirit' (v 46), and breathes his last. Jesus has gone, gone to await his fellow sufferer in the paradise of the Father.

Through this final act of surrender the current of divine mercy begins to flow. Lives change. The Roman centurion standing by the Cross begins to praise God, declaring in the light of all that had happened, 'Certainly this man was innocent' (v 47). The crowds who had come to witness a gruesome spectacle of justice go away beating their breasts (v 48). The tide begins to turn. In the distance, many who knew him, including the women who had followed him from Galilee, stood watching on the fringe of something impossibly new and wonderful (v 49).

Joseph of Arimathea, a member of the Jewish Council, who had dissented from its actions, who was still waiting in hope for the Kingdom of God to come, seeks Pilate's authorisation to bury the body of Jesus (vv 50–51). His hopes were not exhausted, even if this was such an obvious end. The watching women now follow him to the tomb, and go off to prepare the spices and ointments for burial (v 55). Through the sabbath, they rest, with whatever hopes were left to them.

Then the astonishment and confusion in the early dawn of the next day . . . the report of the women to the eleven (Lk 24:9); Peter's amazement after seeing the empty tomb (v 12); the burning hearts of the disciples on the way to Emmaus and their recognition of him in the breaking of the bread (vv 32-35)—and then the appearances of the Risen Lord to the apostles and the community about them so 'that repentance and forgiveness of sins be proclaimed in his name to all the nations . . .' (v 47).

In the exchange between dying Jesus and the dying criminal, the mercy that would enable hearts to change and sins to be forgiven has already begun its work. The great refusal has been reversed. The time of healing love has come.

The Eucharist and Ecology

We are slowly coming to appreciate the planetary significance of the eucharist and its cosmic ramifications—as we celebrate Mass here on planet earth, warmed by the Sun in this corner of our galaxy, the Milky Way, in which 200 billion stars are said to shine. A sense of the interconnectedness of all reality, and of the 'sublime communion of all life', promotes an awareness of relationships, either newly known or long ignored, as with the earth itself, with the biosphere of this planet, within the emergent process of the cosmos itself, and with the sacraments of Christian faith.

This Holy Thursday celebrates a holy communion within a universe of grace and giving. From nature's giving we have the grain and the grapes. From the giving expressed in human work and skill, we have the gifts of bread and wine. In recalling the generous giving of family and friends there is a long history of good meals and festive celebrations. From Jesus' self-giving at the Last Supper, the disciples were given his 'body and blood', the food and drink to nourish life in him. After his resurrection, his giving continues as he breathes into his disciples his Holy Spirit. And working in and through all these gifts and kinds of giving, there is the gift of the Father who so loved the world. So it is that when the Church celebrates the Eucharist, all these gifts come together to nourish our lives in this world in anticipation of the life of the world to come.

The oft-cited phrase found in Vatican II's *Constitution on the Liturgy* refers to the eucharist is 'the summit and source' of the life of the Church.[1] Caught up in the updraught of his ascension, the eucharist of the Church is both a gathering in and a going out, a

---

1. The Documents of Vatican II, *The Constitution on the Sacred Liturgy*, #10.

communion and a mission, a thanksgiving and a hope, an enactment of Christ's presence, and a hope for his final return, as the life of faith opens out to the full measure of the mystery of Christ. By receiving the body and blood of the Lord, Christians lift up their hearts and 'seek the things that are above, where Christ is, seated as the right hand of God' (Col 3:1).

The sacramental economy reaches its paradigmatic form in the eucharist. The risen Lord takes representative fragments of creation, the elements of our earthly reality which nature and history have combined to produce, to transform them into something more, in anticipation of a new totality: '*This* is my body; this is my blood . . .' Jesus' transforming identification with the matter of our world is continued through history as the eucharist is celebrated: 'Do this in memory of me'. In effect, Christ invites his followers to connect with the created cosmos as he has done and continues to do. By receiving the eucharistic gift of his body and blood, we are in fact claiming this world as our own in the way that the Christ already possesses it.[2] By assuming our humanity, the divine Word makes his own the world and the universe to which that humanity is essentially related. The identity of Christ, the Word made flesh, overflows into the corporate identity of the Church as the Body of Christ, in the daily enactment of his words, 'Do this in remembrance of me' (Lk 22:19).

In the eucharist, faith is confronted with the gift that comes with a giving and from a giver beyond any worldly horizon. There are dimensions of height, depth and breadth, of the present and what is to come, inscribed into the eucharist . Appreciating the eucharist and its relationship to life on Planet Earth is not a matter of thinking *about* some religious ritual or even sacramental event, but more a way of thinking from *within* it, by participating in the experience life on this planet within the community of the faith in this time and space.

The cosmic scale of the Eucharist is powerfully evoked in the following paragraph for *Laudato Si'*:

> The Lord, in the culmination of the mystery of the Incarnation, chose to reach our intimate depths through a fragment of matter. He comes not from above, but from within, he comes that we might find him in this world of ours. In the Eucharist, fullness is already achieved; it is the living centre of the universe, the overflowing core of love and of inexhaustible life. Joined to the

---

2. See Anthony J. Kelly, *Eschatology and Hope* (Maryknoll, NY: Orbis, 2006), 187–192.

> incarnate Son, present in the Eucharist, the whole cosmos gives thanks to God. Indeed the Eucharist is itself an act of cosmic love: 'Yes, cosmic! Because even when it is celebrated on the humble altar of a country church, the Eucharist is always in some way celebrated on the altar of the world'.³

In the depth and breadth of the eucharist, the universe is revealed, not as an anonymous fact indifferent to life or death, but as opening into the heartland of God. It presupposes that everything has its part in God's creation and that everything has been owned by the divine Word in the incarnation and involved in the great transformation already begun in his resurrection. All are connected in a universe of gifts and giving, at the heart of which is the self-giving love of God: We are living and dying into an ever larger selfhood: 'Unless a grain of wheat falls into the earth and dies, it just a single grain; but if it dies, it bears much fruit' (John 12:24).. The true self is realised in a network of relationships within a communion pervading the whole of the universe, and shaped by the Trinitarian relationships that constitute the very being of God.

The eucharist as 'thanksgiving' inspires us to welcome the great, generative reality of the cosmos and the ecological reality of our planetary biosphere. To obey Jesus' command, 'Do this in memory of me', is to 're-member' all that has been dismembered in the sterile imagination of modern culture. The Eucharist does not bypass either the universe or our planetary home. Spiritual progress is not an escape from what we are, but a generous reclamation of the world as destined for transformation that hope awaits. We cannot set nature aside, for it is our own flesh and blood. Loving our neighbour means loving the whole cosmic and planetary neighbourhood of our existence. In the measure we share the charged reality of the Eucharist, Christian imagination expands to its fullest dimensions. Paul's prayer begins to be answered:

> I pray that you may have the power to comprehend, with all the saints, what is the breadth and length and height and depth, and to know the love of Christ which surpasses knowledge, so that you may be filled with all the fullness of God (Eph 3:18–19).

---

3. Citing John Paul II, Encyclical Letter *Ecclesia de Eucharistia* (17 April, 2003), 8: *AAS* 95 (2003), 438.

Any celebration of the eucharist necessarily begins with the resurrection of the Crucified (3). It contains a dangerous and provocative memory, not repressing, but proclaiming, the death of the Lord until he comes (1 Cor 11:26)—Paul's wholesome reminder was designed to counter the convivial exuberance of his Corinthians. Ecological awareness, however, cannot but be confronted with the agony of the world and the cost of evolution, with its deaths, extinctions, violence, and dead ends: 'the whole of creation has been groaning in labor pains until now' (Rom 8:22). In the agony and struggle inscribed in nature itself, and ever convulsing human history, Christian hope is wise to focus on 'the Lamb that was slaughtered before the foundation of the world' (see Rev 13:8, 5:6, 7–8, 11–12). It implies that self-sacrifice on the part of God is primordially constitutive of creation itself, and that an aboriginally self-sacrificial divine love is constitutive of divine providence.

By receiving the eucharistic gift of the Lord's body and blood, we are in fact claiming this world as our own in the way that Christ has made it his own. In this way, we become immeasurably larger selves in a world of divine incarnation. The highest moment of communion with God is at the same time the most intense moment of our communion with the earth. For 'the fruits of the earth and the works of human hands' are not magically vaporised by the action of the Spirit. They come into their own as bearers of the ultimate human mystery. Put most simply, in the idiom of John's Gospel, the bread and wine become '*true* food and *true* drink' (Jn 6:55). 'Transubstantiated' in this way, the sacramental reality anticipates the cosmic transformation that is afoot, not as something that leaves the created cosmos behind, but as promising its healing and transformation.

As the source and goal of the whole life of the Church, the eucharist relates us to Christ, connects us with one another, and re-embodies us within the life of planet Earth. Our universe is being drawn into the trinitarian life, toward that ultimate point at which 'God will be all in all' (1 Cor 15:28).

A Forum for Theology in the World Vol 10 No 2/2023

Via Dolorosa: The Path to Calvary

I

From Roman times, the 'Via Dolorosa' defined the path of the condemned criminal from the forum to the place of execution outside the city walls, where the Arch of Gallienus on the Esquiline now stands. It has been long celebrated in Christian piety and devotion in association with Christian martyrs and especially in reference to the *Via Crucis* of Jesus carrying his Cross to Golgotha.

Even if a number of the traditional stations rely more on the pilgrim imagination than on the events recorded in the Gospels, they suggest aspects of the mystery of God's suffering love. Not to refer to them would be to deprive Christian imagination today of the contemplative insights of generations of the saints and sinners who have read and prayed the Gospels before us. For example, the three falls of Christ on his way to Calvary, which figure in the traditional enumeration of the Stations of the Cross, convey a fundamental Gospel truth. It is this: Jesus' surrender to the Father for the sake of the world's salvation, is the result of a choice—on the Father's part in giving us his beloved Son; and Jesus' part, in bearing the whole weight of our human darkness.

Jesus' deliberate act is forged in the harshness of human experience. Among the many places in the New Testament where this is referred to is the occasion when Paul calls the Philippians away from any 'selfish ambition or conceit', and into an attitude of self-forgetfulness in the service of others after the example of Jesus. The apostle cites an early Christian hymn,

> [Christ Jesus] who, though he was in the form of God, did not regard equality with God as something to be exploited, but emptied himself taking the form of a slave, being born in human likeness. And being found in human form, he humbled himself and became obedient to the point of death—even death on a Cross (Ph 2:6–8).

Clearly the way of Jesus was no glorious path of conquest. It was marked at every step with a deliberate and loving self-abasement in giving himself into the darkness and weakness of our human condition. The God he reveals in such lowliness is not a stylised divine being floating above our human world, but one who has compassionately come to meet us, to be with us and alongside us, in the pilgrimage of faith.

II

In this regard, a devotional tradition has depicted three falls of Jesus to evoke three facets of the divine compassion. First, Jesus, as the divine Son, steps out of himself and into this human world: '[he] emptied himself taking the form of a slave'). Second, this divine one is 'born in human likeness', and 'found in human form' in the mystery of the incarnation. He walks with us along this pilgrim way. Third, and this takes us to the heart of the passion, he gives himself up to death, even to the ultimate horror of the Cross, in his vulnerability to the evils of our world: 'he humbled himself . . . to the point of death—even death on a Cross.'

When Christian imagination, then, depicts Jesus falling three times beneath the Cross as he presses on to the final moment, it is sensing the compassionate love that has freely and deliberately given itself 'for us and our salvation'.

If the three falls suggest three aspects of the divine compassion, they also evoke aspects of Jesus' confrontation with the power of evil that reached its culmination on the Cross. His determination to serve the cause of his Father, to give himself for our salvation, was at once a consent to the will of God, and a refusal of all that was less than that. The Gospels speak of his freedom in terms of his being tested by the devil—the embodiment of the false self, and of the idols we so easily serve. It suggests a whole culture that would accommodate Jesus for its purposes, in order to be left it undisturbed.

In the temptation accounts (Mt 4:1–11, Mk 1:12. Lk 4:1–13) in the first place the tempter appeals to Jesus' status as the Son of God to encourage him to turn stone into bread. But the way of Jesus is not to be the Lord of a consumer society, the great provider of material goods. Jesus acted in the name of the God of another way and another life: 'It is written: One does not live by bread alone' (Lk 4:4). In this respect, the whole passion story depicts him as struggling under the weight of the false expectations of the world.

We are taken deeper into the heart of his freedom when he is faced with the possibility of possessing purely political power—'all the kingdoms of the world' (Lk 4:5). The devil offers him 'all their glory and all this authority'. If he would only worship the spirit of this world, 'it would be yours' (Lk 4:7). Again, in the name of the Father who was offering another kind of kingdom, Jesus refuses: 'Worship the Lord your God, and serve him only' (Lk 4:8). The passion is about his struggle against the machinations of political ambition and worldly fame.

In the third temptation the devil entices him to use his divine status to escape from the harsh reality of the world, and so to leave it untouched and undisturbed by the Kingdom of God: 'If you are the Son of God, throw yourself down from here' (Lk 4:9)—the angels of God would be summoned to save the beloved Son from the law of gravity! Against this, Jesus opts to be part of the common human lot, with us in the real world in which God acts. He will not make God an agent of self-glorification: 'It is said, "Do not put the Lord your God to the test"' (Lk 4:12).

III

The way of the Cross suggests further a strange gap in Christian doctrine. The classic solemn definitions concerning the incarnation and the Trinity have formed Christian thinking through the whole of tradition. Nonetheless there was no attempt to define what happened on the Cross and its salvific significance. Though the two-sided paschal event of Cross and Resurrection structures the whole of Christian life, there was no felt need to define the paschal event in doctrinal or dogmatic form. Here, the challenge inherent in Christian existence was not so much to 'define' the mysteries of faith more precisely but rather to inhabit them at the deepest level is of life and commitment.

We contemplate Jesus falling under the weight of a world that has no room for him. or his message. In its thrall to the devil, that world is endlessly creative in making idols for its own glory. It is indifferent to God's glory and resistant to God's will. The freedom of Jesus, in contrast, is found in his exclusive dedication the cause of his Father. That entails obedient self-surrender to the divine will, on its terms. To be for God is to be against all that is less than God. The Letter to the Hebrews makes its point:

> Although he was a son, he learned obedience through what he suffered, and having been made perfect, he became the source of eternal salvation for all who obey him (Heb 5:8–9).

When the imagination of the faith depicts Jesus falling three times beneath the Cross, it is in fact describing the reality of the love of God compassionately giving itself into the reality of our world. Jesus is 'a forerunner on our behalf' (Heb 6:20) to open 'the new and living way' (Heb 10:20). His entire earthly career had followed the direction the Holy Spirit of love.

IV

As Christian devotion imaginatively ponders his last agonised steps and the collapse threatening him after those hours of torture and mockery, the Gospels focus on a number of precious details. It was the Roman custom to make the condemned criminal undergo a final act of public humiliation. The condemned had to carry the cross-beam through the city on the way to the place of execution. This detour was designed to achieve the maximum effect by instructing the populace on the reality of justice. We are told that two criminals were with him on this journey to execution. He was to be in the company of sinners till the end.

As the grim procession of the guards, executioners, official witnesses and the condemned victims wound its way through the Holy City to Golgotha, and as Jesus staggered along in their midst. A foreigner, Simon of Cyrene, is press-ganged into a brutal service. He is made to carry the cross-beam. This man who had migrated to Jerusalem from Northern Africa, is identifiable, at least in one early Christian community, as 'he father of Alexander and Rufus' (Mk 15:21). Simon's forced participation in this horrible event enacted would bear fruit. The significance of the mystery at work in the pain and disgrace of this journey to crucifixion would be recognised by his sons. But at this time, all that was visible to the Cyrenean was the blood-covered criminal on his way to execution.

It is surmised that Simon had been coming in from a farm in the countryside to rest for the Sabbath and to prepare for the Passover feast. Then, this brutal imposition banished any hope of rest and festivity as local authorities picked him out as foreigner for a grisly public service. Whatever slender reputation he may have had previously would be forever tainted by this debasing involvement. Simon's moment of history was one of public humiliation, and to be forever associated with a condemned criminal and the gruesome reality of this crucifixion and the Cross he was forced to carry. He was not to know then that he would be remembered as the father of Alexander and Rufus.

Why did Simon attract the guards' attention? Was he the victim of racial prejudice—an African in Jerusalem? Or was he simply someone so insignificant that no one could possibly object to his being treated in this manner? Had he shouted some word of sympathy, been too curious, or was he simply randomly picked out of the crowd pressing about? These questions can never be answered, even if they remain always worth asking, at least in later times when the non-persons of our societies have no rights and no honour amongst us. Any society set against the truth of God ends by making victims of its own people. Admittedly, all we really know is that he, Simon of Cyrene, was *there*—in the wrong place and at the wrong time; and that he was considered capable of carrying the Cross of the condemned man. The Gospels are silent on any further details. Little wonder, however, that believers over the generations have thought of Simon as unwittingly doing what we all are called to do: 'Whoever does not carry the Cross and follow me cannot be my disciple' (Lk 14:27).

The Cross seems always to occur for us in a jagged, random way. No time is ever the right time for any of us to be pulled out of ourselves by the demand to follow Christ. His Cross is offered in the face of the suffering other who meets our eyes, and permits no escape from the question, 'What will you do now when you are the only one here to help me?'. Our plans and calculations are interrupted with the dreadful otherness of God's will and the demands of our suffering neighbour. If the Cross came to us only as something we could plan, only as a demand we could accommodate, only as enabling us to maintain our present undisturbed self-sufficiency, it would not be the Cross at all; nor would it be love for others on the terms they need us; nor surrender to the Lord whose kingdom is not of this world. It is a burden and demand taking us beyond where we would plan to go. It finds us all when, like Simon, we too have finished our work and looking forward to some rest and festivity, to confront us with the demands of a love that will not let us rest or rejoice until we act. And even then, it means finding rest in another kind of peace and another kind of joy. It leaves us feeling foolish and ill-prepared . . . but in good company. St Paul writes to his enthusiastic Corinthians,

> For I decided to know nothing among you except Jesus Christ and him crucified . . . But we speak God's wisdom, secret and hidden, which God declared before the ages for our glory. None of the rulers of this age understood this: for if they had, they would not have crucified the Lord of glory . . . (1 Cor 2:2–8).

V

The Gospel of Luke records that 'a great number of people' (Lk 23:27) followed after Jesus on his way to execution. Perhaps they recognised in him something of themselves—their best selves, exposed and condemned in harsh dark world of human pride. The anonymous crowd can be taken as a symbol of all innocent nameless victims of history who had followed and will follow him along this path— whether he is known to them or not. Amongst these are found the women 'who were beating their breasts and wailing for him'. These especially were pierced by the tragedy that was taking place. They wondered at the kind of world in which they had given birth to their children, where the best and most beautiful values of our humanity are at the mercy of other murderous realities—a world in which neither humanity nor God seemed to count when it really mattered. They lamented the impending execution of this man who had offered them another hope. He had loved their children, seeing in them the tender promise of another kind of life. For him all arguments about who was the greatest was a silly distraction. He had placed one of their children by his side and said, 'Whoever welcomes this little child in my name welcomes me . . . for the least among all of you is the greatest' (Lk 9:46–48). He stood for a world hospitable to the powerless and the innocent, in which their children would be safe. They could recall the time when they had brought their children to him to receive his blessing, how his disciples, locked into the serious business of their own ambitions, had tried to discourage them. But he had called their children to him and insisted that they be allowed to come, for to such as these who had not learned the ways of violence and ambition 'the kingdom of God belongs' (Lk 18:16). To his mind, 'whoever does not receive the Kingdom of God as a little child will never enter it' (18:17).

Now that hope was finished, and the age-old violence of the world was about to crush him, returns to them, and utters words that seemed horrible contradiction to what he had promised before:

> Daughters of Jerusalem, do not weep for me, but weep for yourselves and for your children. For the days are surely coming when they will say, 'Blessed are the barren, and the wombs that never bore, and the breasts that never nursed' (Lk 23:28–29).

Some dreadful reversal of even the most precious forces of life was taking place. The lamentation of these women was a lament for a lost world which had failed to recognise its salvation: 'For if they do this when the wood is green, what will happen when it is dry?' (v 31). If Caiaphas had calculated that it was better for one man to be sacrificed to Roman justice for the sake of peace, there would come a time when those same Romans would make a similar calculation. It would be better for this whole nation to be sacrificed for the sake of the empire. The temple would be destroyed and Jerusalem would be razed. If his own people had turned to Jesus in a way of peace and surrender to God, the kingdoms of violence would have been subverted from within. But now the politics of violence and envy and victimisation will go on . . .

What will happen . . .? There would be greater darkness yet, and the sorry tale of the world's desolation is not yet over. What light would be left to shine in the coming darkness? All the mothers of all the children who have seen their children die, forgotten in the fierce priorities of war, racial violence, political ambition and greed have felt the darkening of the world. Jesus has meant another world to them; and now he was going to his end. What hope was left? The promise of a kingdom open to the powerless and the innocent 'like little children' had no place in a world forged by self-serving power.

In the light of what did happen, Christian devotion would imagine two further scenes not mentioned in the Gospel, both dealing with Jewish women who felt the full extent of the tragedy that was taking place. The first recalls how a certain Veronica wipes the face of Jesus, and further legend has it that the imprint of his face was left on the cloth. There is a deep evangelical truth hidden here. By allowing ourselves to be called out of our isolation and to meet the eye of a suffering other, by meeting Jesus in the least of his brothers and sisters, his image is impressed on us, and we are conformed to Christ in his love.

The second scene is Jesus' meeting with his afflicted mother. It is as though devotion cannot wait till the moment when John's Gospel will present her as standing by the Cross. Here, too, a deep Gospel truth is evoked. As the Father gives what is most intimate to himself for world's salvation, his Beloved Son, it is the vocation of Mary, the first disciple, to show forth the boundless love of God in her maternal love, that a new humanity might be born out of such travail. She had lived with the prophecy of Simeon that her son would be 'a sign that would be opposed so that the inner thoughts of many would be revealed' (Lk 2:34–35). Now the opposition was coming to its climax, and the violence that rules our world was brought into the light, and the ways of hope were to be deprived of every support other than the truth of God. In her surrender to what only love could bring about, Mary's heart is torn: 'and a sword will pierce your own soul too' (v 35). Thus, she becomes the model of the compassionate love which, by following Christ as the only way, learns how to wait on God, and not to be turned to hatred and despair in the midst of darkness.

The love welling up from the Father and expressed in the Son confronts evil through the Cross. But such love is not defeated, diminished or changed into something else when it meets the full force of evil. Love is unconditional. Though Jesus, the Son of the Father, is rejected, condemned and executed, the love that he embodied kept on being love, 'to the end' (Jn 13:1b). Far from being changed into hatred or resentment, God's love outstrips all human limits and contradictions. In this, it outwits the wisdom of a world built on revenge and retaliation. The light of love is not overcome by the darkness of evil (Jn 1:5). By suffering the Cross, the love of Christ shines in its true radiance even at that darkest point. The excess of evil is met with the greater excess of love.

VI

Through the mystery of the Cross, God claims even the dreaded realm of death to display an extreme of generosity as though love has absorbed the menace of death into itself. Death no longer appears as a fearful barrier cutting us off from life, and from the God of life and love. Death now is revealed as the extreme to which God's love has gone, and the Cross becomes the revelation of divine compassion and mercy. By being exposed to the power of evil and by not being overcome by it, the 'Lamb of God takes away the sin of the world' (Jn 1:29). The Lamb who was slain (Rev 5:7) has become the 'atoning sacrifice for our sins . . . but also for the sins of the whole world' (1 Jn 2:2).

Though Christ's love unto death for 'his own in the world' (Jn 13:1), history's vicious circle of loveless-ness has been arrested. It is replaced by a new movement, that of an opening circle of love and reconciliation: 'If anyone does sin, we have an advocate with the Father, Jesus Christ the righteous' (1 Jn 2:1b). Faith is familiar with the conflict between an ever-vulnerable love and the violence of human selfishness. Followers of Jesus are summoned into a life of genuine loving: 'We know love by this, that he laid down his life for us – and we ought lay down our lives for one another' (1 Jn 3:16). Love is to be lived out, not as a sweet emotion, but in the sober realism of sacrificing ourselves in the service of others. In this. the demands of love are always excessive. But our loving, however hesitant or defective, lives from the prodigality of that love that goes beyond all human limits: '. . . we will reassure our hearts before him whenever our hearts condemn us; for God is greater than our hearts . . .' (1 Jn 19–20).

A Forum for Theology in the World Vol 10 No 2/2023

Good Friday

The solemn reading in the liturgy of Good Friday is introduced as 'The Passion of Our Lord Jesus Christ according to John'. It tells a too familiar story, until we appreciate it as the love-story of God's immersion in our world. It tells of a terrible cost, in terms of pain, sorrow, failure and forgiveness. Any great love costs a life: 'Having loved his own who were in the world, he loved them unto the end . . .' (Jn 13:1).

Despite betrayal and denial on the part of his disciples, despite the mockery and rejection of others, and then the condemnation, torture and execution inflicted by those who ruled his world. A story of appalling tragedy, yet, according to John's Gospel, not without hints of majesty. It draws us into a centre of peace in the storm of suffering, where the love not of this world knew what it was about, beyond anything that world could imagine.

There are as many ways of hearing this story as there are people and the different ages of human history. Countless generations have listened, and found in their different experiences that here was the whole and healing truth.

The Good Friday liturgy allows us simply to behold Jesus, and look even at each other, with a heart disarmed. It brings home to us that the way of the Church is always a movement toward the Cross where the passion of God is on display. It invites us to feel the depths of suffering that so often hides inarticulate—in each of our lives, in the Church itself, in the world at large.

'Behold the wood of the Cross on which hung the Saviour of the world'. The Cross is unveiled in order to touch our hearts, as the faithful are invited to venerate it with a kiss, a touch, a genuflection or a bow. The eyes of faith see the Cross against the backdrop of all our questions, fears and hopes.

By contemplating the wounded body hanging there, we are in the presence of the fathomless Love that has reached out into creation to find each one in this moment. Whatever the darkness, a light has begun to shine. Faith is not peering into a void marked only by a Cross, but is meeting the gaze of the Love that has been revealed. It has kept on being love, and never been changed into something else—never less that itself, and ever more than the heart dare imagine. The Cross shows Love exposed to death, not as its defeat, but as the limit to which such love t has gone.

The eyes of faith see the Father through the image of the Crucified Son as the original Love that inexhaustibly gives itself into the ruthless dynamics of the world. Love keeps on being love as an ever-more tender compassion and unreserved mercy. As the Cross of Christ points up to God, its arms point out to the world.

We see embodied in the crucified Jesus the whole agony and pain of our world. Enfleshed in him are all the sufferings of the innocent, even the more dreadful sufferings of the guilty, for he bore our sins.

He too dwells in the shadow of death, and goes through the bitter valley of suffering. All our human solutions seem useless if we dare make eye-contact with even one of the uncounted millions who have gone down in defeat. We think of those whose lives seemed to have met up with unbearable tragedy. Beyond them, in the grim regions of suffering and isolation there are the nameless crowds of the slave camps, of the mass graves; and then, the starving children, the poor, the tortured—the detritus of history.

Yet here too the Cross is grace as it jolts us out of ourselves into the immense family of human suffering. It demands that we bear one another's burdens. It serves as a signpost for the path along which we fear to travel and give ourselves. Unless Jesus had gone before us and known the regions we most fear, we are left alone with our lost selves—toward those places and people where hope has no voice unless it is ours:

> for I was hungry and you gave me food, I was thirsty and you gave me something to drink, I was a stranger and you welcomed me, I was naked and you gave me clothing, I was sick and you took care of me, I was in prison and you visited me (Mt 25:34–36).

'We adore you, O Christ, and we praise you, because by your holy Cross, you have redeemed the world.' The Cross is fixed into the hard rock of the world. Love speaks in the words of the crucified One whispers his word of hope, 'Come to me, all you that are weary and carrying heavy burdens, and I will give you rest' (Mt 11:28). The veneration of the Cross in the liturgy of Good Friday is always a moving scene. The generally big crowd, larger than the usual congregation, come up, often awkwardly, to kiss, touch, or bow before this rough memorial to a man crucified long ago.

In our different ways, we who take part in this strange procession, sometimes barefoot, witnessing to a love that has reached out and found us in the deepest and darkest areas of suffering and evil. The parables that came from the lips of Jesus turned the ordinary world turned upside-down, calling into question the hitherto unquestionable systems of worldly power and status. He was intent on calling the world out of its desperately self-destructive ways into a universe of grace and mercy.

In him, the world is being made new, and the very meaning of time has changed: a transforming love was at work; the form of life without end had begun;

the world was being renewed. Before that event, what people most valued was always at the mercy of what they most feared.

The dreadful power of evil and the finality of death held sway over the course of time. God's raising up of the Crucified shocked time into another shape. Many who share with us this time under the sun still consider that history runs on, forever inconclusive and undecided as eras of progress or decline come and go. There is no final goal, no reign of God.

Many revere this Jesus of Nazareth one of the many good people, who despite a noble vision, were eventually found out by the harsh reality of the real world. His resurrection, if it means anything, is just a poetic way of saying that goodness will out in the long run. A nice thought; but history remains a catalogue of horrors and defeats. The dead stay dead; and rising from the dead is no solution for the world's ills. For Christians, the crucified and risen Christ is the light of the world. He embodied a love stronger than death, stronger too than those who use the threat of death for their purposes.

In the light of the resurrection, the terrible Friday of condemnation, torture, defeat and execution is now known as the *Good* Friday—the astonishing revelation of an all-merciful love embracing the world at its darkest level. In that light the shocking scandal of this death is understood as the revelation of the transforming power of God's love. In that light, the longest day of hopelessness, the Saturday of grief and desolation, with Jesus, dead and buried, became known as Holy Saturday. He had visited the world of the dead and brought release to all Jesus was not the victim of a blind fate or of a capricious divine will.

The Father in sending his Son, was not intent on entering the world as one more earthly power. The true God was not intent on taking revenge and putting down all opposition. The God whom Jesus represented was otherwise.

Who *this* God was, what serving *this* God meant, how *this* God valued human beings—especially those considered worthless in any social and cultural system—were questions answered the terminal moment of the Reign of God that Jesus proclaimed. Execution by crucifixion was employed by the Roman authorities precisely because of its obscene impact. The system would not tolerate anyone who dared to question it. As a result, the Cross had to be scandal to all Jews, including the first disciples. The God they served had promised mighty works of vindication and liberation. But this?

Inevitably, too, it was sheer folly to the Greeks. Their philosophy could never imagine such pitiable vulnerability on the part of the divine being who ordered the whole of cosmos. Needless to say, the Roman imperial authorities found any suggestion that God could be identified with a criminal they had executed to be deeply subversive of the power of Rome.

Yet St Paul defiantly insisted that the 'foolishness of God', acting in this shameful death, was the source of all wisdom: 'for the foolishness of God is wiser than men, and the weakness of God is stronger than men' (1 Cor 1:25). There is nothing morbid or voyeuristic as the early Christians 'proclaimed the death of the Lord until he comes' (1 Cor 11:26); there is an unflinching realism in their accounts of what took place.

The Gospel of Mark depicts the agony of Jesus as intense isolation as he is offered the cup of complete earthly failure. The world bears down on him as utterly opaque to the light of God. There is no sign of the Father's presence: 'His soul began to be greatly distressed and troubled' (Mk 14:33). He falls to the ground, praying that the hour might pass. He feels the infinite weight of the world's fate . . .

Luke will add the graphic detail of the bloody sweat (Lk 22:44). In this state of utter collapse, with his disciples asleep and the triumph of his enemies impending, he is stripped of everything except his character as Son. Nothing else remains as even the disciples flee. This terminal moment wrings from him an act of unreserved surrender to the One from whom he came: 'Abba, Father, for you all things are possible, remove this cup from me; but not what I want, but what you want' (Mk 14:36).

The Father is the God of the unlimited possibilities . . . of love.

The Son's compassionate solidarity with all who resist evil and struggle in the cause of good, embraces all in a love and mercy beyond anything the human mind can imagine. The Kingdom will come on its own terms and in its own time.

Peace that the world cannot give: 'Put your sword back into its place. For all who take the sword will perish by the sword' (Mt 25:52). Yet a sorry cycle of betrayal and abandonment. One of Jesus' disciples, Judas, betrays him to the parties plotting for months to destroy him. They hand him over to the Jewish leaders. From the Sanhedrin he is taken to the Roman governor. Pilate passes him along to the local puppet king. Herod sends him back to Pilate.

The Governor offers him to the mercy of the mob.

> And so, betrayed by one of his own, denied by the leader of those he had chosen to walk with him, left for lost by the rest of them, despised now by his own people, libelled by false witnesses, he is condemned in the courts of the secular and religious authorities of his time. Then, after being tortured by the police and soldiers guarding him, he is taken to be executed in the hideous manner of crucifixion.

Throughout the whole drama of Jesus' condemnation and execution, it is as though the powers of evil are defying God to reveal himself.

God would not be God if the Kingdom that Jesus proclaimed ended in futility. And it would be worse than failure if the Father's intention to save and forgive was changed into vengeance and some worldly power-play.

To answer evil with evil, as though the law of 'an eye for an eye and a tooth for a tooth' guided God's own behaviour, would be the flat contradiction of all that Jesus stood for. Yet there is no divine vengeance. Love does not turn to hatred and revenge. God is no self-serving worldly power. The Father sends no legion of angels. For the God of Jesus has refused to have any presence in the world save that of the crucified Son. And, as this Son prays for the forgiveness of those who have crucified him, he rejects any worldly identity, any worldly justification or protection, save what can be found in an ultimate mercy. In venerating the Cross, faith recognises Jesus as the victim of a world that barricades itself against the call of love and justice. Violence is the ultimate decider; hope is left with nothing but what God can be and what God can do.

In such a world—for the salvation of such a world—God has to be revealed in a way never been known before. The God of the Cross, of self-giving love, the God of those who trust that the world can be otherwise . . . Though Easter bathes everything in its light, hope is never an escape.

Under the sign of the Cross, hope is earthed in time and space and caught up conflicts of history. To live such hope means exposure to a world that cannot allow itself to be called into question:

For it, love, forgiveness, peace and the justice that these promise are impractical; and those who think otherwise are a disturbing presence. Though Christians must love the world as God loves it, they are ill-advised to expect that the world will love them back.

As Paul writes, we are 'always carrying in the body the death of Jesus . . . for while we live, we are always being given up to death for Jesus' sake, so that the life of Jesus will be manifest in our mortal flesh . . .' (2 Cor 4:11).

The Cross may seem an odd icon for the World Youth Day. The *joie de vivre* of the young, their optimism, enthusiasm, even innocence compared to those who have known too much of the world's evils, all gather under the sign of the Cross something too dark, ugly and sorrowful to inspire the youthful heart?

But at stake is a deeper question: is the youth of the Church to allow itself to be carried along and swallowed up by the spiritless routines of the world as it is? Or are these new generations to see themselves as agents of a new beginning? Dare they defy the hatred, greed, violence and lust for power that are taken for granted as the way things are, and must ever be?

Someone must grasp the nettle—in this case the Cross of Jesus, the enduring icon of the end of an old world and of the beginning of a world forever new.

A Forum for Theology in the World Vol 10 No 2/2023

Befriending Death

Death is an obvious dimension of life on this planet and a condition for its evolution. We must give death its due if we are to appreciate the beauty and wonder of terrestrial life. After a century and a half of evolutionary science, we can begin to understand the randomness, contingency, and terrible costs of evolution in the 3.8 billion-year history of life on this planet? Ecological destruction of planetary proportions is the subject of widespread lament and anxiety. In contrast, there is another sense of diminishment as in the words of the Johannine Jesus: 'Unless a grain of wheat falls into the earth and dies, it remains just a single grain; but if it dies, it bears much fruit' (Jn 12:24). Here, an inevitable and even positive sense of diminishment is subsumed into the ultimate hope for transformation and communion.

It remains, however, that death is the price to be paid for the evolution of life on earth, making possible the emergence of differentiated, complex living beings in a world of wonderful biodiversity. Unless we belong to the mortal world of life on this planet, human beings would never have come into existence. Moreover, there is a sober, scientific backdrop to the death of individuals and species, the eventual collapse of the solar system, even if billions of years from now. And that will entail the extinction of all planetary life. The law of entropy is built into the cosmos itself.

In the meantime, though human history has always known its catalog of natural disasters, famines, earthquakes, plagues—'acts of God'. We now live with the eerie possibility of death-dealing human activities affecting the planet in the era of the Anthropocene. Biological warfare, thermonuclear incineration, and ecological destruction still menace life on this planet. Huge technological systems shape the ecological, social, political, and economic world. The consumerist economy is insatiable in its demands. Enormous military arsenals at the disposition of dozens of governments openly include weapons of mass destruction designed for biological or thermonuclear warfare. This range of lethal capacities is the material expression of a readiness to wipe out whole populations if the necessity arises. Given that the possibilities of mega-death are taken for granted in the contemporary environment, the Christian spiritual task is to draw attention to the mystery of life, its source and goal.

Indeed, the dread of death goes some way in explaining morbid aspects of modern culture. Obsessive consumerism, deracinated individualism and careless destruction of the environment, all alike arise from the failure to give death its due. As creatures, we are immersed in the totality of nature, connected to it, caught up and carried along by it. Authentic life arises only by accepting the limitation and contingency of our existence within this universe, yielding ourselves into ourselves into the stream of life and death. The human person is caught between inevitable limitations on our being in the world, and, on the other hand, openness to the uncanny gift of life and existence.

Faith is contemplative in its reverent openness to the mystery of creation and the Creator. It exercises, also, a redemptive effect in causing human beings to be less driven to self-destruct, and more disposed to realise the divine image in the works of love and justice. The authentic self, therefore, is realized in its connectedness with all creation—in contrast to the tiny scope of the fear-driven, illusory self, fabricated by denying death. The true self emerges only by befriending the mortal character of existence in true humility. Our human being is earthed, grounded, bound up with the immense dynamism of nature into whose processes we are each and all immersed. Humility connects us to the whole, immersing each and all in a wondrous universe of gifts and giving. And out of humble acceptance of mortality and the de-centring of the self can come the wisdom to coexist on this planet as "our common home."

And yet death is shrouded in a darkness deeper than the inevitable termination of biological life. Death, Paul declares, is the 'wages of sin' (Rom 6:23). The implication is that death is the consequence and manifestation of sin—alienation from God, and the refusal of communion—with the Creator, and creation. It is the choice for self-centered ego against all others. As a result, the seemingly natural fact of death becomes the carrier of a profound sense of rupture and guilt. It looms through life as 'the last enemy' (1 Cor 15:26).

The more human existence is turned in on itself, the more it occupies a shrinking universe. In that self-centred world, I exist by competitive self-assertion against the Other. In this respect, death is the deepest threat. Death holds no promise of life; it is the carrier of all that is meaningless and threatening to the life we have made for ourselves

And yet life contests the reign of death as total, for ordinary lives know sudden impulses of wonder, nameless hope, and the exhilaration of great loves, just as all are humbled before the strange grandeur of moral achievement. In such moments, there is an uncanny, death resistant 'more' in the experience of the mystic, the artist, the martyr, the prophet, the thinker, the scientist, and the activist. There is an intimation of eternity-in-the-making. The thrust of human life is toward fulfillment—*in*, and even *through*, death. The dynamics of personal existence that moved and motivated life in its normal course have been largely hidden from consciousness, only to surface at the moment of death into full awareness. The full dimensions of our being unfold. In this respect, the self dies out of the limited individuality of the ego, into a more deeply relational form of being. This is to become aware of itself within the universal whole.

And yet, this unfolding is most deeply a meeting with God, the boundless Other who has been present in every stirring of existence. The deepest mystery of the Creator has worked within all the elements and causes that have formed us, our earth, our universe. In the light of God, we are brought to a moment of final decision, whether to accept God and the totality of creation, allowing ourselves to be carried along by the flood of life, and being and belonging, toward an eternal fulfillment.

Going to God does not mean merely escaping from the earthly existence in which we lived and in which Christ has been our earthly brother. Rather, ultimate fulfillment must include this earth redeemed, transformed, and brought to fulfillment in God, all in all.

Here, Christ, crucified and risen, is the focus of faith and hope in the all-creative mystery of compassionate and transforming love. The death of Jesus was indeed deadly. It occurred as failure, betrayal, isolation, condemnation, torture, and execution. God's love felt the force of the human problem of evil. However, the love that gave itself to the end (Jn 13:1) was not defeated by the power of evil. For the death of the crucified Jesus enacts and embodies the ultimate form of life as he surrenders himself to the Father in solidarity with the defeated and the lost. The ultimate point of Christ's self-offering reveals God as a love stronger than death. In Christ, crucified and risen, those receptive to the divine Gift are summoned to pass from a self-serving existence into the God-centred realm of eternal life, already inaugurated in the gifts that will last—faith, hope and love (*cf* 1 Cor 13:13).

Death remains as the limit of this form of earthly life, but as then transformed into an act of ultimate self-surrender—to the Father in union with Christ, and in the creativity of the Spirit. The entropy affecting each individual biological existence is dissipated to allow for a higher realization of communion, in relationship to the 'all' and participation in the whole. The individual self becomes a wave of communion, a truly relational self. The upward vector of ascent for the human being moves from electrons, to atoms, to molecules, to proteins, to cells, to organisms, to the complexity of the human brain, and to the cosmic overture of human consciousness. In all this, the direction of life is one of transformation in increasingly rich and complex relationships. In this respect, death cannot mean terminal dissolution but rather the expansion of the self into its fullest relationality. Death would not be an alien intruder, but a relative— 'Sister Death', as St Francis could pray—within the cosmic promise of the fullness of life in Christ.

Only a transformation of our whole embodied existence can answer the hopes written into life. By participating in his rising from the tomb, the entropy and limiting individuality of biological life, is definitively overcome. In him a new creation is anticipated in Christ 'the resurrection and the life' (Jn 11:25). The realism of this new creation is expressed in all four Gospel narratives in regard to the empty tomb. It is the historical marker of the cosmic transformation that has begun in Christ: 'So if anyone is in Christ, there is a new creation: everything old has passed away; see, everything has become new!' (2 Cor 5:17).

Hope nonetheless remains hope. It lives always in the in-between of what is, and what is yet to be, as it waits on the mystery of final transformation. Even the New Testament writer soberly concedes, 'As it is, we do not yet see everything in subjection to him' (Heb 2:8f). Yet for all the sobriety of Christian hope, the great conviction remains firm. In Christ, the universe has been changed. Death has been radically 'Christened'. Christ did not die out of the world, but into it, to become its innermost coherence and dynamism. Indeed, in his death, resurrection and ascension, the mystery of the incarnation is complete. For the Christian, dying in Christ is to be conformed to the crucified and risen One, in order to be newly embodied in the future form of cosmos itself: 'The last enemy to be destroyed is death ... When all things are subjected to him, the Son himself will also be subjected to him who put all things under him, that God may be all in all' (1 Cor 15:26–28).

All mortal existence is poised, therefore, over an abyss of life. The empty tomb, a sign of the creative power of the Spirit, is of cosmic significance. It suggests the full-bodied reality of resurrection, and seeds history with questions and wonder as to what great transformation is afoot. The empty tomb, so soberly recorded in each of the four Gospels, offers no salvation in mere emptiness. It functions as a factor within the awakening of faith as a new consciousness of life unfolds. It moves, first, from the empty tomb, discovered as a puzzling fact. It then awakens to cosmic surprise over what had happened, for Jesus appears as newly and wonderfully alive: 'Do not be afraid. I am the first and the last, and the living one. I was dead, and see, I am alive forever and ever' (Rev 1:17–18). Then faith returns to the tomb as an emblem of the new creation. From there it expands into the limitless horizons of a transformation of all things in Christ. Such faith is not primarily looking back at a death, but facing forward into the promise of eternal life, in a universe transformed.

Christian theology is focused in the paschal realism of Christ's death and resurrection. It offers no super-theory to explain death away. Questions necessarily remain. First, is our theology sufficiently humble? There can be no theological theory or ecological system that controls death, nor any egomaniac subjectivity able to appropriate death to its purposes. Inscribed into the course of our lives is an elemental rupture; and any expression of hope that represses the lethal force of death is not starting from scratch. A beauteous sense of nature or the wonder of the universe unfolding through its billions of years cannot camouflage the finality of death in all living things. Theologians may find themselves offering a guided tour of the world of eschatological fulfillment, but to no avail. In the face of death, all must "wait in a condition of openness toward miracle and mystery, in the lived truth of creation."[33]

In other words, are we really letting ourselves and others—even Jesus himself—really die? In our Easter celebrations, we may have been too inclined to hurry past the caesura of Holy Saturday. The liturgy graphically portrays this in the stripping of the altars and emptiness of the tabernacle. It drives home a basic truth: before death can mean resurrection, it must mean being dead—even for Jesus himself. He went down into the realm of the dead, as in the words of the Apostles' Creed, he 'descended into hell'. The Crucified was dead and buried. Christian hope is not a video replay of highlights once the team has won. In Holy Saturday, a healing providence makes time for all our human griefs and lamentations, in a world of apparent God-forsakenness, failure, and waiting for God to act in God's appropriate time; in God's own way. Jesus was not only dead, but buried, descended to the depths of universal dread. To hurry past the deadly reality of the Cross to a kind of automatic resurrection would obscure the need for a time of waiting before that Friday can be affirmed as 'Good' and that Saturday as 'Holy'. Only by waiting on that unfolding, can the imagination be christened, and hope expand beyond repressive optimism to its authentically God-centred character.

The horizon of hope is shaped by Christ's self-giving unto death for the sake of the world's salvation. This gift occurs so that 'by the grace of God, he might taste death for everyone' (Heb 2:9), and 'free those who all their lives were held in slavery by the fear of death' (Heb 2:14–15). In the gift of Christ, a multi-dimensioned giving is at work: Christ gives himself in death for the salvation of the world; and the Father so loves the world as to give the Son into such a death (Rom 8:32; Jn 3:16). The gift of the Spirit breathes faith into the mortal existence of Christ's followers: 'Those who believe in me, even though they die, they will live' (Jn 11:25). The crucified and living One embodies the ultimate life-form: 'I am the first and the last, and the living one. I was dead, and see, I am alive forever and ever; and I have the keys of Death and Hades' (Rev 1:18).

Though hope relies on the God whose love is stronger than death, it has the realism to admit that 'in the days of his flesh, Jesus offered up prayers and supplications, with loud cries and tears, to the one who was able to save him from death' (Heb 5:7). The God of life has acted. But the Father did not save Jesus from death, but vindicated and glorified him in his death for others by raising him to a new order of life. As the form and source of new life, he is the firstborn from the dead (Col

1:18). In the light of his death, hope looks through death and beyond it. But it does so, first, by being a way into it—in union with Christ in his death: 'Since, therefore, the children share flesh and blood, he himself likewise shared the same things, so that through death he might destroy the one who has the power of death' (Heb 2:14). To be united with him in his death is to share his victory over all the demonic forces that work in human culture through the threat of death.

By sharing in his death, hope is already sharing in his resurrection (*cf* Rom 6:3–5). Still, hope remains hope. It is never immune to the darkness of life. It must show its own patience. It means waiting for the mystery of love to prove itself stronger than death and all the demonic powers that use the threat of death for their purposes. The New Testament expresses a sober realism:

> As it is, we do not yet see everything in subjection to them, but we do see Jesus, who for a little while was made lower than the angels, now crowned with glory and honor because of the suffering of death, so that by the grace of God he might taste death for everyone (Heb 2:8–9).

There is a further edge at which theology trembles: the mystery of God. Though the holy and immortal God does not die, there is something about the way God is God, about the way the Trinity is these three self-giving divine persons, which leads death into the deepest darkness of all. This deeper darkness is not a threat, but an intimation of life in its trinitarian and most vital dimensions. Union with Christ in his death is most radically self-abandonment to the Father. It yields to the incalculable creativity of the life-giving Spirit. It means incorporation in the Body of Christ. In this Trinitarian frame of reference, a self-surrender is inevitably asked of each mortal being. But that is to share in the unreserved self-emptying of the divine three in relation to each other, and to the world which they have created and drawn into their communal life. Death, in this respect, is the last, and perhaps the only truly genuine act of adoration of the God whose life is self-giving love. Only by dying out of the cultural and biological systems and projects structuring this present existence are human beings remade in conformity with the self-giving and communal trinitarian life of God.

Befriending death means greeting 'Sister Death' in the great conversion inherent in the firmness of faith, in the surrender of hope and in the desire of love.

Holy Saturday: The Longest Day

I

Homilies do not often refer to Holy Saturday. Pastors and parishes are understandably getting ready for the Easter Vigil. Besides, Christ's 'Descent into Hell' is the most puzzling article of the Apostles creed. But hope needs to take its time. It must make time to dwell on this longest day when Jesus is truly dead among the dead. On this Saturday, he is indeed dead and buried, is cut off from the land of the living. And, it must seem, left undefended even by God. Jesus of Nazareth is just one more executed criminal, gone from this world in failure and shame.

Unless it pauses here, our hope can veer in the direction of mere optimism. It begins to repress both the horror of the real death of Jesus and the dreadful extent of human tragedy. To hurry past this Saturday to the triumph of the Sunday suggests that his death simply means resurrection. But that is to deny both the deadliness of his death—and our own. It is better, then, to let our Alleluias be silent, the altars lay stripped and the tabernacle stand empty than to settle for a hope untouched by grief. For without the ability to grieve, there is no capacity for joy. On this day, Jesus, and ourselves with him, are stripped of everything save what God can be and what God can do in God's good time.

There is a truth hidden in the silence and grief of this Saturday. Jesus is one with us, not only on the surface of life, and not only in the experience of life's mortal agonies. He has also gone down into the underworld of the dead. With the burial of that tortured body, God-ward direction of our lives comes to a dead-end. And so, before we Christians dare call this day 'Holy Saturday', we must first feel something of the unholiness of what has happened. The Alleluia of Easter rings true only if it has groaned under the weight of failure, guilt, and desolation at the absence of God.

In other words, this day was first of all an 'unholy Saturday'—a day when nothing is happening, nothing had changed. God was apparently powerless to save even his Innocent One. All we can do is grieve and wait . . . and wonder if God can still act; and if so, when and how?

Very simply, we must allow ourselves to be provoked into the contemplation of the brutalised corpse of Jesus; and, with that, to recall the dreadful finality of the deaths of all those we have loved and cared for. For this middle day was originally experienced as not being the middle of anything. It was the day of God's obvious defeat and banishment from the world, and reduced to silence. Though Jesus had offered an amazing hope, now the hearts of his disciples were benumbed in a universe turned suddenly grotesque.

The Apostles Creed speaks of his 'descent into hell'. The Latin word used was *inferna* or *inferos*— the lowest places that human imagination can depict. It evokes that point of God-forsakenness where hope is most tempted to despair. Jesus has gone down into these regions of ultimate dread, the point most distant from God. There, darkness reigns, words run out, and death is at its deadliest.

The Word has indeed become flesh, not only on the surface of life, but right down to its most dreaded depths. The last great cry of Jesus from the Cross contains all the inexpressible dread of our humanity in the face of impenetrable mystery. It echoes in all the deaths of those who trusted in an apparently powerless God. Yet, in his descent into hell, Jesus embodies the outreach of God, embracing the dead, the hopeless, the irretrievably lost.

God so loved the world. The Father has given what is most intimate to himself, the beloved Son, into the point furthermost from him. Love has gone to the end. The communion of love between Father and the Son has been stretched to this extreme point. Only then can love become a compassion limitless enough to contain every dimension of our human existence.

On Holy Saturday, hope finds its proper depth. Philosophers and theologians may speculate on how God acts in our human freedom. But in Jesus' burial among the dead, hope is given an image through which to sense inexpressible dimensions of God's mercy. Human beings can pervert their God-given freedom—as when they crucified Christ himself. But even if the rebellious die cursing God as the great rival, the story does not end there. God's love is not changed into vengeance, nor is the Father's mercy diminished.

The silence of Holy Saturday echoes with the words of hope. The realm of death is not annihilation, not ultimate isolation. Jesus is there. The region most distant from life and furthest from God is not beyond the reach of the Father's love.

Moreover, there is that realm of ultimate damnation: 'hell'. It comes into existence as 'the second death' (Rev 20:14), but only if these dead refuse the salvation that is offered them. The God they rejected in the times of their proud self-sufficiency now comes to them in the depths of their weakness and need. They are offered a way out of their loveless self-enclosure through the love that has found its way in. And so, the healing of purgatory can begin.

We are merely saying what St Paul has already said. There is 'nothing in all creation, nothing in life or death, nor things present, nor things to come, nor height nor depth, nor anything else in all creation able to separate us from the love of God in Christ Jesus' (Rom 8:38).

On Holy Saturday, we meditate on the love that has led Jesus to be dead with the dead. In owning its grief, in facing its dread, hope is most alive.

II

Over seventeen centuries ago, an unknown preacher posed a question to his hearers about the meaning of this day:

> What is happening? Today there is a great silence over the earth, a great silence and stillness, a great silence because the King sleeps; the earth was in terror and was still, because God slept in the flesh and raised up those who were sleeping from the ages. God has died in the flesh, and the underworld has trembled.[1]

---

1. The second reading from the Office of Readings for Holy Saturday, The Divine Office II,(Sydney: EJ Dwyer, 1974), 320–321 (PG 43, 440A–452C).

The great hopeful conviction of Christian hope was forged in the face of a terrible ending. The body of the dead Jesus lay hanging on the Cross.

If the corpse of a crucified criminal were left exposed it would have desecrated the Sabbath festival (Jn 19:31) and polluted the land. In this case, it is the crucified Jesus who is hanging there; in his life, condemned as a subverter of the Temple worship; in his death, a potential defiler of the Holy Day. Both enemy and friend wanted him buried. In the event, Pilate gave permission to Joseph of Arimathea to take away his body:

> So Joseph took the body and wrapped it in a clean linen cloth and laid it in his own new tomb which he had hewn in the rock. He then rolled a great stone to the door of the tomb and went away (Mat 27:59–60).

The great stone was rolled into place. Devout women watched. But the Jewish authorities prevailed upon Pilate to set a guard over the place of burial: 'So they went with the guard, and made the tomb secure by sealing the stone' (Mat 27:66). Jesus is dead, buried, laid to rest in a rocky grave which his disciple, Joseph, had excavated for himself.

In a cosmic sense, Jesus lies buried in all our graves. Can any hope survive? Can any new hope spring forth? Though Christians will, indeed, come to live in the joy of an answer to these questions, what was then clear is that hope had to take its time. It must wait through the whole length of this longest day when Jesus is truly dead among the dead—dead and buried, cut off from the land of the living, an executed criminal, gone from this world in failure and shame, knowing no divine vindication.

The liturgy of this day prescribes that our Alleluias be silent, that the altars of our churches lay stripped and the tabernacle stand empty. If our sorrow is to be turned to joy, hope must learn how to wait, to express the grief out of which it is born. On this day, we are stripped, along with Jesus, of everything save what God can be and what God can do in God's good time.

This day of waiting extends through the whole of human history. A great stone is lies heavy on the graves on the uncountable dead. Human history has witnessed the killing of many martyrs. So many hopes have been buried. The tombs of peace-makers have always been carefully guarded. Their spirits must not escape to accuse the violent of their crimes. What had they been hoping for?

Holy Saturday: The Longest Day

In all the imagination of great art, in all the inspiration of poetry and music, in all the fervour of religious faith, what have we been waiting for? Have we been simply fabricating images of ourselves to compensate for a void of meaninglessness? Are our hopes merely projections of ourselves thrown onto a blank screen for fear that there is no answer, no meaning, no final truth? Is faith merely setting up one more idol in history's crazy hall of mirrors? Or may we really see in the crucified Jesus an icon, the face of the living God, back-lit by a light not of this world, holding us in a loving gaze?

Hidden in the silence and grief of this sabbath when the hopes of all the world are at stake is the conviction that Jesus, the beloved Son, is one with us not only on the surface of life, not only in the experience of life's mortal agonies, but in going down into the underworld of the dead. With the burial of that tortured body, the God of Jesus too is apparently buried. Where have our hopes gone?

With Jesus dead and buried, the image of his Father is blotted out, and the power of his Spirit reduced to the impotence. Where is God now? Jesus lies in the grave. He had proclaimed the reign of God, a realm of grace in which God would lift up the poor and the outcast. But that kingdom has not come. With Jesus dead and buried, one more hopeless failure has been added to the sum of hopeless failures, those who failed to adapt to the way things are and ever will be. The poor have possessed no Kingdom; the mourning have received no comfort; the meek have not inherited the earth; those hungering for justice are still famished; the merciful have found no answering mercy; the pure of heart see no God in this place of burial; the peacemakers remain God's orphaned children; while those persecuted in the cause of goodness have made no difference . . .

Jesus is buried in a black hole. Faith and hope and love, all the deepest God-ward direction of our lives, are swallowed up and brought to nothing.

In contemplating the brutalised corpse of Jesus, our hearts cannot but recall the dreadful finality of the deaths of all those we have loved and cared for. For this Saturday, this middle day, was originally experienced as not the middle of anything. It was the day of God's obvious defeat and banishment from the world. The Word is reduced to silence. All those who had once thrilled in wonder at the promise he gave are now numbed and bewildered in a universe turned bleak and grotesque.

III

In the language of faith, the believer professes faith in Jesus Christ as the 'only Son' of the Father and as 'Our Lord', who 'conceived by the power of the Holy Spirit and born of the Virgin Mary', enters the world not only as a human being with us, but as one who 'suffered under Pontius Pilate, was crucified, died, and was buried'. A Cross and a tomb in the Palestine of a particular time under a particular Roman administration mark the fact that he lived, died, and was buried at *that* time, in *that* place. But the creed goes on. Jesus has been with us not only on the surface of life, not only in the agony of suffering and disgrace, not only in the grave, but to a mysterious further extent: 'He descended into hell.'[2]

What is this hell which Jesus goes down into? 'Hell' translates the Greek *Hades*, the god whose name is 'Unseen', ruling over the underworld. The word, hell, is often used to translate the Hebrew *Sheol*, meaning literally 'the place of questioning'. The realm of the dead has always left the human mind wondering, appalled at the fate of those who gone from this life. The Old Testament describes it as the abode of 'darkness', 'silence', 'dust', 'the place of no return', a total separation from life and, indeed, even from God (*Cf* Job 7:9). It was an underworld of inaction and lifelessness (Eccles 9:10), of sadness (Sir 14:11–17), of powerlessness (Isa 14:10), and even of no praise of God (Ps 6:5; Ps 88:3–6, 16). Linked with the Canaanite imagery of *Mot*, the god of death, it was the place where the dead were 'swallowed up' and 'devoured' (Isa 5:14). Death's appetite is never satisfied (Prov 30:16). All life's radiance and power come to nothing (Isa 14:10f).

More soberly the Latin of the creed, *inferna*, or *infera*, seems to mean simply 'the lowest places' that human imagination can depict, the depths of God-forsakenness in which we have no obvious human hope. Jesus has gone down into the regions of ultimate dread, the point most distant from God. He has entered a darkness that leaves the imagination appalled, where all theories are useless, where death reigns unchallenged in all its lethal power to silence, to separate and destroy.

Jesus, in surrender to the Father's will, descends to the point furthermost from God. He dies as one accursed, condemned by the

---

2. See the *Catechism of the Catholic Church* (Homebush, NSW: St Pauls), 49 and 164–165.

Law of Israel, rejected by his own people, executed as a criminal by the imperial power, seemingly abandoned by the God whose reign he proclaimed—his prayers unanswered, his disciples scattered.

As the Son sent into the world's heart of darkness, he has gone down to that depth where death reigns as the final scandal in a world of suffering, and as the focus of the human problem of evil. Jesus goes down—'goes under'—enters into the doom of being dead in the world of the dead, fettered in 'the pangs of death' (Acts 2:24).

Haunting the silence of this day when Jesus lies buried is the question, Can the ultimate love he proclaimed reach him, and those who follow him, at this impenetrable depth? Does his tomb sealed with the great stone set the final limit on all life and love, even on the power of God?

But God works. The Word must become flesh—right to the end, and be reduced to utter silence. The communion between Father and the Son is stretched to breaking point. The love that God is shows itself to be infinite compassion for the lost. The Father sends his Beloved Son into this realm of apparent God-forsakenness. Nothing can span that distance except the Spirit of a love that knows no bounds. Only if such love can survive at the most deadly point of death can it promise a new creation.

In his descent into darkness, Jesus becomes God's way of reaching out to the dead, to the hopeless, to the irretrievably lost. In his descent to this depth he brings all the compassion of God. The Father has given what is most intimate to himself, the beloved Son, to the point furthermost from him. Love has gone to the end.

Truly, he goes to seek out our first parent like a lost sheep; he wishes to visit those who sit in darkness and in the shadow of death. He goes to free the prisoner Adam, from his pains, and his fellow-prisoner, Eve—he who is God and Adam's Son . . . 'Awake, O sleeper and arise from the dead, and Christ shall give you light!'[3]

IV

The sense of this point of ultimate enigma and dread is conveyed in the many references (over fifty) that the New Testament makes to Jesus being raised 'from the dead', *ek nekron*. The mystery of Holy

---
3. From the homily already quoted, The Divine Office II, 321.

Saturday lies in Jesus' total obedience to the Father's will. He goes down into these most dreaded, deepest reaches of human darkness. He is with the dead in all their powerlessness.

On this day, hope begins to rally at the point where all seems lost. It begins to rise up through the way that love has opened. While philosophy and theology will always puzzle over the manner in which the freedom of God respects our human freedom, in Jesus's death and burial among the dead Christian hope finds an image of the inexpressible creativity of divine love. Human freedom, even in a state of ultimate perversion, even when it is frozen in resistance against the power and claims of the infinite Other, now finds that this Other is with it in unreserved forgiveness. Love continues to offer itself even when it is most rejected. Christ is *inferno profundior*, 'deeper that the lowest place' (Gregory the Great). In his death, Jesus has gone down into the realm of the dead, down into that silence and failure of the dead and the lost.

However we human beings, with our burdens of guilt and dread, imagine this lowest place to which Jesus descends on this longest day, faith can now share the conviction of St Paul,

> For if we have been united to him in a death like his, we will certainly be united with him in a resurrection like his. We know that our old self was crucified with him so that the body of sin might be destroyed, and we might no longer be enslaved to sin. But if we have died with Christ, we believe that we will also live with him. We know that Christ, being raised from the dead, will never die again; death no longer has dominion over him. The death he died, he died to sin, once for all; but the life he lives, he lives to God. So you must consider yourselves dead to sin and alive to God in Christ Jesus (Rom 6:5-11).

The place of ultimate estrangement is now open to another presence— the only presence that could penetrate it—that of an absolute love giving itself, as the Father so loves the world as to give his only Son. The compassion of God fills all the dimensions of human existence: 'God was in Christ reconciling the world to himself, not counting their trespasses against them . . .' (2 Cor 5:19). The dimensions of the Cross span the whole abyss into which we can fall. The Lord of life has been there; even there. Jesus has changed the realm of death into a place of meeting. No part of our experience, no corner of the universe is closed to an all-merciful love. Love moves through the whole of creation to offer hope where no hope was to be found.

> I am your God who for your sake became your son, who for you and your descendants now speak, and command with authority those in prison: Come forth; and those in darkness, Have light; and those who sleep, Rise.
> I command you, `Awake, sleeper. I have not made you to be held a prisoner in the underworld. Arise from the dead. I am the life of the dead. Arise, O man, work of my hands, arise, you who were fashioned in my image, Rise, let us go hence.' For you in me, and I in you, together we are one undivided person.[4]

To the eyes of hope, Jesus is buried that he might ascend, to fill the heights and the depths of created world: he 'fills all things', descending even to the 'lower parts of the earth' (Eph 4:6). He is Lord of the dead, and holds in his hands the keys of death and Sheol (Rev 1:18). Every knee bows to him, even those 'under the earth' (Phil 2:10). The Son of Man, three days and three nights in the heart of the earth, is Jesus, the new Jonah (Mat 12:40). Though he is swallowed up by the monster of death, though he descends into the abyss (Rom 10:6–8), against him the gates of Sheol shall not prevail (Mat 16:18; 27:51–53). He has the power to subject death as the last enemy (1 Cor 15:26–29). After his death, he preaches to the mysterious 'spirits in prison' (1 Pt 3:18–20), and to all the dead (4:6). Freed 'from the fetters of death' (Acts 2:24), he is 'the firstborn of all creation' (Col 1:15)—'the first-born from the dead' (v 18).

Through him, the loving compassion of God is extended throughout the whole universe. By descending into the realm of utter darkness, he dies into the heart of the world to open it to grace:

> For in him all the fullness of God was pleased to dwell, and through him to reconcile to himself all things, whether on earth or in heaven, making peace by the blood of his Cross (Col 1:19–20).

---

4. From the same homily, *The Divine Office II*, 522.

As this boundless love stirs in our hearts to unsettle our familiar versions of hope and despair, it leads us to declare that the Friday of crucifixion was indeed 'Good'; and that this Saturday, this longest day of waiting, is indeed 'Holy':

> The cherubim throne has been prepared, the bearers are ready and waiting, the bridal chamber is in order, the food is provided, the everlasting houses and rooms are in readiness, the treasures of good things have been opened; the kingdom of heaven has been prepared before the ages.[5]

---

5. Conclusion of the homily quoted above, *The Divine Office II*, 522.

The Empty Tomb

The biblical data on the resurrection of Jesus includes an ambiguous indicator, namely, the fact of the empty tomb. Its discovery is connected to a temporal reference to 'the third day'. There is also a personal connection as well, since 'some women of our company' discovered it (Lk 24:23). It never suggests, however, either for the disciples, or for those who would profit from their testimony, that the reality of the resurrection was founded on the mere emptiness of the tomb. A vanished corpse is not the same as the Risen Lord. Nor does an unoccupied grave mean a transformed creation. In fact, the discovery of the empty tomb initially gave rise only to perplexity and fear (*cf* Mk 16:8; Lk 24:5, 11). The women, confronted with the absence of the dead body of Jesus in the tomb, were exposed to a new form of questioning, 'Why do you seek the living among the dead?' (Lk 24:5a).

There is no implication that the early witnesses to the resurrection either haunted a grave or lingered among the dead. If believers neglect the significance of the empty tomb, there are inevitable negative consequences. The phenomenon of the resurrection would be left at the mercy of those who would prefer to be undisturbed by such an event. Christ's rising from the dead would tend quickly to become a nice thought in a world in which nothing had really changed; and in which the resurrection could not *really* happen. Moreover, it would mean dismissing the special role of women in communicating the Gospel of new life. After all, unless it were utterly sure of what it was reporting, the Gospel would hardly base its case on the testimony of women in a culture that scarcely accepted their credibility.[1] For

---

1. NT Wright, *The Resurrection of the Son of God* (Minneapolis: Fortress Press, 2003), 607–608.

that matter, neither friend or foe pretended that the tomb contained the remains of Jesus. One Gospel writer at least is quite aware of the allegation that the corpse had been stolen (Mt 28:1–15). This was a quite predictable reaction on the part of those for whom, for whatever reason, Jesus had to stay dead and buried.

The empty tomb serves as an historical marker for a transcendent mystery. Right there, set within the history of human defeat and failure, it recalls Christian faith to defiantly full-bodied in its realism. The empty tomb leaves its trace in time and space and matter, thereby suggesting that there are far more surprises in store than scientifically predictable events can allow. It sows a seed of wonder and questioning in the ground of the material cosmos.

The empty tomb focuses faith at the clear edge of a new world in the making. What is coming to be, what has begun with Jesus rising from this tomb, goes beyond all desperate efforts to reduce the 'real world' to the overweening assumptions of violence, pride and greed: 'He has put down the mighty from their thrones and exalted the lowly' (Lk 1:52).

The world of the past is classically wrapped in a fateful melancholy. The inscription on the ancient tombstone read, *et in Arcadia ego* ('I too was once in Arcady'). Virgil expressed it with immemorial poignancy: *sunt lacrimae rerum et mentem mortalia tangunt* ('tears are at the heart of reality and every death-bound thing affects the way we think'). A kind of all-pervading sadness is never far from the power of violence. It is a dismal concession to the loss of all ultimate hope. Yet both the defeats of melancholy and the pretensions of violence stand under the divine judgment of life to the full.

In contrast, the raising of the crucified Jesus from this tomb remains a scandal to all the desperate systems that would reject the power of God to transform the world. If his tomb is not empty, the creative force of the crucified and risen Jesus is easily accommodated to mythic fantasies of whatever kind. Easter becomes a meaningless holiday and a marketing opportunity for chocolate eggs. Unless that sepulchral space is left empty, the resurrection of Christ is either lost in a mystical vagueness or replaced by a self-centred rationalism. And so, however stupefying this emptiness is, it must be critically guarded. Nature abhors a vacuum; and the monuments to power and triumph begin to tilt dangerously when there is an empty space at their foundations.

The mind must 'seek understanding', but first of all it must be receptive to what is given to be understood. The Word became not theory, not myth, but flesh—with all the contingencies and particularities that this implies. The raising of the dead-and-buried flesh of Jesus from the tomb is designed to serve the manner in which God, untrammelled by earthly conditions, has acted. Something of cosmic significance is being revealed when Jesus is transformed in the totality of what he was when laid in the tomb. The matter that made up his crucified body is transformed. His tortured corpse has been changed into his full-bodied risen existence. It must have appeared as the least promising material for the glory of God to be revealed, for his corpse is the remains of man who had been executed in defeat, humiliation, and apparent abandonment by the God in whose name he had acted.

Aquinas remarks that Jesus' risen body is not an imagined reality (*corpus phantasticum*), but the God-wrought embodiment of the saving Word.[2] His death is not the result of the entropic forces of nature which lead to decay. It figures in the way God has acted 'to show forth the divine power' (*ad ostensionem virtutis divinae*).[3] In this 'showing-forth', the resurrection and the empty tomb belong together in the concrete particularity of the divine way of acting. Jesus' proclamation of the Kingdom of God led him to defeat, condemnation, and execution. He was crucified, dead and buried. His vindication by the God he so intimately invoked as 'Father'. But that did not mean that came down from the Cross; nor that he walked out of the tomb to rejoin his distraught followers in life as usual. He came to them in a new realm of existence. For that reason, there is a certain appropriateness—or *convenientia*, as the Scholastics would say—in the transformation of his crucified body. It occurs to display, in an anticipatory manner, the Spirit of God at work.

God's power is in no way constrained by the defeats, condemnations, violence and burials that mark the human history embodied in this man. Jesus rose to face his disciples who had looked on him transfixed on the Cross (Jn 19:37, *cf* Zech 12:10). The Lamb who was slain retains the marks of the Cross even in his risen body. In his total physicality, he is given to faith in a form that anticipated

---

2. *STh* 3, q 54, a. 1.
3. *STh* 3, q 51, a. 3.

a new creation: 'I was dead, but now I live forever and ever' (Rev 1:18). He had been done to death as the witness and agent of God's reign. His blood had been poured out for the new covenant. He has previously been present to the disciples who had had every reason to fear that death—for him and even for themselves—would result from his head-on confrontation with the violent powers of politics and religion—when left with only God to defend him. Their fears were justified, as they mourned the execution that eventually occurred. His dead body was the gruesome expression of his failed mission, of his prayer unanswered and of his Father's defeat. For God to raise him from the tomb of disgrace and defeat would manifest the scope of a divine victory over the powers of death and violence that had, so they thought, terminally rid themselves of him. His tomb would become a provocatively empty space in the fabric of the world that had done away with him.

There is, then, a unique realism in this economy of salvation. God has acted in history, not by communicating a new idea, but by doing a provocatively and properly divine thing. Through Jesus' transformed physicality, the divine intention for the whole of creation is anticipated and manifested in this exemplary instance. As a result, the world is no longer a total system of entropy and decay, nor a theatre in which the scripts of self-justifying violence are enacted. Even though death is still our common fate, its dominion has been disturbed. The risen Christ is the first and last letter, the 'alpha and the omega' (Rev 22:12), of an alphabet by which the great poem of the Word comes to expression. A love stronger than death has been revealed.

He Is Risen

> When it was evening on that day, the first day of the week, and the doors of the house where the disciples had met were locked for fear of the Jews, Jesus came and stood among them and said, 'Peace be with you'. After he said this, he showed them his hands and his side. Then the disciples rejoiced when they saw the Lord. Jesus said to them again 'Peace be with you. As the Father has sent me, so I send you.' When he had said this, he breathed on them and said to them, 'Receive the Holy Spirit. If you forgive the sins of any they are forgiven them; if you retain the sins of any, they are retained' (Jn 20:19–24).

It was now toward the end of that day of astonishing good news. The stone had been taken away, the tomb was empty, the wrappings of death had been unwound, Magdalene had come with her wonderful message. And yet that day was ending, and darkness was returning. Despite the joy of the disciples, the powers that had crucified him were still abroad. He has ascended to the Father, but they were still where they always were. He had gone into glory, but they were locked in their old fears. He had escaped from death, but had they? He was changed, but how changed was their world?

Into the locked room of this fear Jesus now comes. He stands among them and gives them the greeting of peace. On one level, it is the *shalom* of normal Jewish greeting; but now it means something more. His previous words spring into new life:

> My peace I give you. I do not give to you as the world gives. Do not let your hearts be troubled, and do not let them be afraid . . . You heard me say to you, 'I am going away, and I am coming to you' (Jn 14:27–28).

Standing in their midst, he is the embodiment of the peace not of this world. Their hearts, once crushed and broken with fear and grief, now open to a new gift, the peace of the Risen One among them. His departure from them in death is now revealed as a new coming to them in a peace that no human violence can negate. Yet, for his disciples there would still be the fear of persecution in a world antagonistic toward him and them; they, and the future generations of believers would continue to be faced with their own frailty. But in his peace there was fundamental assurance. The peace of his presence would continue, no matter how troubled the times would be. He had come 'that you may have peace. In the world you will face persecution. But take courage; I have conquered the world' (14:11).

He who had conquered the world now comes to these who were still very much in the world. Yet he comes from beyond death—from where death was no longer the all-limiting power. He comes in the power of the reign of God. He comes as the bearer of forgiveness. Neither the evils we suffer nor the evils we cause are the last word anymore.

He shows them the wounds in his hands and his side (v 20). The marks of the Cross have become radiant signs of life crying out to God for resurrection. His wounds are a judgment on the powers of evil that had been unleashed to do away with him, but are now shown up in their powerlessness. The scars of the nails and the spear are now emblems of a life so endless and abundant, so founded in God, that the wounds of death could be displayed as a badge of victory. In the wounds of the crucified Jesus, now risen and present to them, the disciples saw that our human existence, despite all its struggle and pain and violence, is capable of a redemption. For the human story of violence is now subverted from within. The Cross of Jesus was the Trojan horse in which the irresistible powers of God's peace, forgiveness and love lay concealed.

> It was fitting that God . . . in bringing many children to glory should make the pioneer of their salvation perfect through suffering . . . For this reason, Jesus is not ashamed to call them brothers and sisters . . . Since, therefore, the children share the same flesh and blood, he himself likewise shared these same things, so that through death he might destroy the one who has the power of death, that is, the devil, and free those who all their lives were held in slavery through fear of death (Heb 2:11–15)

'Then the disciples rejoiced when they saw the Lord' (Jn 20:20). Their sorrow had been turned into joy. The crucified one now lived, and the joy of the life he embodied overflowed from him, and brimmed over within them: 'I have said these things to you that my joy may be in you, and that your joy may be complete' (15:11).

Jesus speaks again: another greeting of peace from the Risen Lord (20:21). Peace must keep on being peace in the lives of the disciples. From now on, peace received must be peace given to others, in a life of peace-making. As the disciples enjoy the peace of Jesus' presence and thrill with the joy of his life, they must enter now into the outgoing movement of his mission. As he has been sent by the Father, they are sent forth by him: 'As the Father has sent me, so I send you' (v 21). The open circle of love and life expands. As branches of the living vine (15:5), they are to bear fruit in the world in witnessing to the truth of the love that has been revealed. The peace of Christ is a peace open to all in a life of communion with God . . .

But the atmosphere of the locked room still holds a sober memory of the fear and defeat in which the disciples had been enclosed. So now Jesus breathes another Spirit into them. This Holy Spirit had been given as the last breath of the Crucified to Mary and John at the foot of the Cross. Now it is given to the expanding Church of the generations to come: 'Receive the Holy Spirit . . .' (v 22)—the Breath of a new holiness, of a new peace and unity for humankind in God . . . In the power of this gift, 'if you forgive the sins of any, they are forgiven them . . .' (v 23). Having received the gift of merciful love, the disciples are to be its agents in the world. The forgiveness they had received in the peace and joy of this moment would now be the forgiveness they will communicate to all who would receive it.

'If you retain the sins of any, they are retained' (v 23). At first, this would seem almost a mean restriction on the joy of this new beginning. But these words of the Lord remind his followers that the peace he gives is not a false peace. It is not a pretence. It does not cover over deceit, hatred and human pride. Love will not settle for anything less than freedom in those to whom it is offered. It will not be used as a convenient consolation for those who would come to God on their own terms. Love will allow anyone to deny the truth.

The breath of holiness which Jesus communicates to his disciples demands that they confront the world, contesting the violence that rules it, to name its crimes and to stand with its victims. Sent by Jesus, his followers are now agents of the Spirit who 'proves the world wrong about sin and righteousness and judgment' (16:8). If the world is to receive the gift of God's love, our self-justifying ways must yield to another judgment. For the world to deny Jesus—whom it crucified as a criminal but who is now risen from the dead—would mean for it to be hopelessly locked in the domain of death. Christians, in the world yet not of it, in the peace they offer and the truth they tell in Christ's name, are the bearers of another life. It promises no peace and no joy, but only disturbance and judgment, to those who hide in darkness from the light that now shines. The Risen One upsets the self-enclosed world; and neither its judgments nor its tombs can hold him.

The resurrection of Jesus does not distract faith into an otherworldly domain. Believers must engage their world in its reality—which will include persecution for them and a continuing resistance to the truth of Christ himself. Yet despite the inevitable conflict and risk that threaten, 'the darkness is passing away and the true light is already shining' (1 Jn 2:8). From the Risen One, an expanding circle of community unfolds to include all peoples, and even the whole of creation. The disciples are sent into the world with the consciousness of being part of the new humanity already realised in Christ. To share in the humanity of the Risen Jesus means to receive and to offer the love and forgiveness we have received. Violent relationships based on envy and vengeance are abolished as Christ explodes the vicious circle of all our hatreds. Even the emblematic antagonism existing between Israel as 'God's Chosen People', and the rest of the nations of the world is healed at its root. Peace has broken out. St Paul, in his letter to the Ephesians, in reference to the healing peace that Christ is for all, proclaims

> For he is our peace; in his flesh he has made both groups into one, and has broken down the dividing wall, that is the hostility between us . . . So he came and proclaimed peace to those who were far off and peace to those who were near, for through him both of us have access in one Spirit to the Father (Eph 3:14–18).

Into that locked room of all our fears Jesus has come. The Spirit has been breathed forth. For the disciples there is peace and rejoicing as the energies of new life begin to stir; and they are sent by the Risen One into the world with the power of new life. They had seen the Lord.

But Thomas had not been there with them (Jn 20:24). As he enters into this room luminous now with the wonder of what had taken place, he holds back—and states his own conditions for believing: 'Unless I see the mark of the nails in his hands, and put my finger into the mark of the nails and my hand in his side, I will not believe' (Jn 20:25). For him the stone was still enclosing the corpse of the crucified and the binding cloths of death still wrapped him round. The dark reality of the tomb still chilled the heart of this disciple. Like Mary Magdalene before him, Thomas was still clinging to Jesus in the conditions he has known.

Believers from earliest times have found in this disciple called 'the Twin' (v 24) something akin to their own hesitations and fears. Thomas is related to us all when we find ourselves insisting that the Risen Lord must fit into our limited worlds, and not we into his . . .

One week later, once more on the 'Day of the Lord' as the earliest generations of Christians would call their Sundays, the disciples are gathered behind closed doors, and the recalcitrant Thomas is with them. And so is Jesus. He comes and stands among them, again with his greeting of peace. He confronts Thomas; and in loving sympathy for the hesitations and ambiguities which all generations of believers know, Jesus then offers to meet the conditions his apostle had imposed: 'Put your finger here and see my hands. Reach out your hand, and put it into my side' (v 27). And yet, the Risen One utters the summons to go further, 'Do not doubt, but believe' (v 27).

Now all Thomas's conditions fall away. In an ecstatic act of faith, he leaves behind all the criteria he had imposed on how God could act. The stone is removed from his heart; the wrappings of death are unwound; the tomb is empty. This moment in this room, as every moment in every place where believers gather, is filled with the presence of Crucified and Risen One. In the ecstasy of faith, Thomas goes beyond the world of his own calculations to enter the universe of deathless love and unbounded grace: 'My Lord and my God!' (v 28). Here, now, he finds the Word who was "in the beginning", the Word who was 'with God' and 'was God'. The disciple sees how the Son of Man has been lifted up to be revealed as 'I am he' (8:28), as the unique revelation of the Father. All his past experience of the master he had followed and of the God he had sought to serve come together as he recalls the words of Jesus, 'The Father and I are one' (10:32). He has come 'to know and to understand that the Father is in me and I am in the Father' (10:38). In Jesus he finds his Lord and his God.

Though Thomas had borne the burden of our human hesitations, the ever-present Risen Lord invites us all into the full freedom and joy of true faith: 'Blessed are those who have not seen, yet have come to believe' (20:29).

The Crucified is risen. He is present to the Church in the water and the blood of baptism and the eucharist. He has breathed into his disciples the Holy Spirit to send them into the world as he was sent, into a world that we now experience as certainly larger and perhaps more threatening than the world of ages past. But when the present experience of believers is illumined by meditating on the word of Scripture, they enter into a holy communion made up of many witnesses: like the Beloved Disciple, we receive Mary, the first of the disciples, into our home. Likewise, Peter experienced the misery of his own weakness and came to confess the Lord, that we might find new courage. Magdalene, too, found her way from grief to joy, the disciples overcame their fear, and the resistance of Thomas fell away—that we might continue to believe, familiar with both their darkness and their light.

In that great communion around the Risen Jesus, the words of one of these first believers find their way into our hearts, these twenty centuries later:

> We declare to you what was from the beginning, what we have heard and seen with our eyes, what we have looked at and touched with our hands, concerning the word of life—this life was revealed and we have seen and testify to it, and declare to you the eternal life which was with the Father and was revealed to us—we declare to you what we have seen and heard so that you may have fellowship with us; and truly our fellowship is with the Father and with his Son Jesus Christ. We are writing these things so that our joy may be complete (1 Jn 1:1-4).

The universe transformed

> Rejoice, heavenly powers, sing, choirs of angels! Exult, all creation around God's throne! Jesus Christ, our King, is risen!
>
> Rejoice, O earth, in shining splendour, radiant in the brightness of your King! Christ has conquered! Glory fills you! Darkness vanishes forever![1]

---

1. From the Exultet, the Liturgy of the Easter Vigil.

As the Exultet sings every Easter Vigil, the whole of creation rejoices. The power of the resurrection already touches everything in the universe. In and with the risen Jesus the earth rejoices, clothed in the brightness of eternal communion with God. In the depths of all creation, the heart of the Risen One is the centre of a new vitality. It is the heart of love; the pulse of new, ultimate life beats there. In him the whole of creation awakes to find itself to be heaven-in-the-making.

While the body of the Risen Lord is no longer visible and palpable in the ordinary conditions of biological life, he has not ceased to be incarnate in the world of God's creation. The whole of creation is contained in the risen humanity of Christ, even though the full glory of this event is yet to be revealed. Paul prays that the Christian community of Colossae will show the patience and joy appropriate to the great transformation that has occurred:

> May you be made strong with all the strength that comes from his glorious power, and may you be prepared to endure everything with patience, while joyfully giving thanks to the Father, who has enabled you to share in the inheritance of the saints in light. He has rescued us from the power of darkness and transferred us into the kingdom of his Beloved Son, in whom we have redemption, the forgiveness of sins.

This illumination of mind and heart, and the sense of wonderful release flowing from the resurrection are graces affecting not only our human relationship to God, but also our relationship to everything—the whole of creation. In the risen Lord, the whole universe has been called home:

> He is the image of the invisible God, the firstborn of all creation; for in him all things in heaven and on earth were created... He himself is before all things, and in him all things hold together (Col 1:11-17).

Christ Jesus remains still embodied in the cosmos, as "the firstborn of all creation", even though he is no longer subjected to the conditions of earthly life. To a new and final extent Christ is present in the totality of the world. When the scriptures speak of him as "Lord", "Head", "the New Adam", "the firstborn of all creation", "the first born from the dead", these early documents of faith present him as "before" all things, the one in whom all reality coheres and find its fulfilment: "all things hang together in him" (Col 1:15). Not only has the merciful love of God broken through to our world, but our world, irrevocably united to him, breaks through to its ultimate destiny. In him "the end of the ages has come upon us" (1 Cor 10:11). St. Ambrose captures this cosmic sense of the resurrection in his statement, "In Christ, the world has risen, heaven has risen, the earth has risen".[2]

Today, in the knowledge science has given us, we stand in wonder at the great cosmic process that has brought us forth over an unimaginable expanse of time. The COBE satellite has given human eyes the sight to peer back fifteen billions years to our cosmic beginnings. We can have some sense of the blazing fireball of our cosmic origins, as it unfurls into billions of galaxies, and condenses into the elements which at this moment are firing the energies of our brains and the beating of our hearts, in all our happy capacities to wonder and to hope.

We are the first generation to have such a vision of the origin of our universe. In accepting such a past, we understand ourselves, despite our different histories and life-stories, to be united in the fifteen billion year old story of the emergence of the universe. Our "common clay" is now recognised as stardust, a cosmic fall-out uniting human, animal, plant and mineral as the outcome of a great cosmic event. Phosphorus formed in the heart of the stars gives us the skeletons that structure our bodies. The stellar iron enters our blood. The sodium and potassium that drive signals along our nerves are part of a larger message. The cosmic flame of hydrogen burns in our brains. Carbon molecules fuel our metabolism. Our lungs breathe an inspired past...

Such is the prelude to any appreciation of the amazing creativity of our own planet Earth. To look back over those four and half billion years to the origin of our planet is to witness a vast cauldron of activity in which the basic chemicals necessary for life were brewed. As this elemental matter slowly cools to crystallise and condense, it combines and complexifies until some marvellous point is reached at which primitive life emerges in the oceans. Out of these oceans come, in their time, creatures of the shore, of estuaries and marshes, to spread eventually over dry land, to take root in the soil, to float or fly in the air, to move on paw or hoof or foot in their various habitats,

---

2. Ambrose of Milan, De Excessu Fratris sui I, 2 PL 16, 1344.

each to occupy a special in the life of our planet. Finally, there comes the human, the most complex arrival in the amazingly productive history of the earth.

The universe rejoices, then, in all the marvellous leaps and transformations that have taken place within it. Our specifically human history has been a long, creative struggle against the forces of entropy and death. We human beings are always living beyond ourselves in hope for a more complete life. Despite the biological cycles of birth and death, we typically seek to bequeath to generations to come the enduring meaning and values without which life would not be worth living. The true and the good and the beautiful are the proper domain of the human spirit. The individual is supported and nurtured in families, groups, societies. Physical sounds and signs break forth into languages and literatures in a world of teeming communication. Art transforms the worlds of sight and sound, of shape and colour and movement, into the entrancing forms of music, dance, sculpture and painting, poetry and drama. Pacts between primitive tribes slowly and painfully inspire the demand for a world-order of justice and global peace. Science accumulates the capacity to transform our physical environment in a thousand ways. The comparative self-enclosure of the primitive world opens into the stream of global human history, as we face the challenge to become one people on this one small planet.

Yet despite all the achievements of art and science, of thought and culture, we have here no lasting city. Death continues to mock human achievement, and our highest aspirations have to deal with the overwhelming forces of human evil and self-destruction. Human freedom is continuously being checked, frustrated, appalled by that over which it has no power. The physical laws of mortality and the historical movements of progress and decline assert themselves as a negativity against which we are powerless. The universe can seem so essentially indifferent to human achievement, so uncaring of the individual destiny or cultural attainments that our greatest sages can see it all as vanity with "nothing new under the sun" (Eccles 1:9). Death as an inescapable biological fact comes to symbolise all that is alien, hostile, radically insensitive to the varied creativity and fulfilment to which we might aspire. It is all doomed to an eventual and total collapse. Does diminishment, death, exhaustion conquer all?

In the resurrection of the crucified Jesus human hope finds a final assurance. Another energy is at work—a limitless love that "nothing in all creation" (Rom 8:38) can resist or diminish. God "is not the God of the dead, but of the living" (Mk 12:27).

The God of the living, the God who has so loved the world, is decisively revealed in an event that affects the whole universe of our existence. The resurrection of the Crucified has a cosmic effect. In Christ's rising from the dead a universal transformation has occurred. What we most cherish is no longer at the mercy of what we least value or what we most fear. True life has been revealed as stronger than death. At the heart of the universe, there is the energy of an infinite love. St Paul sums up this gracious sense of the universe: "All things are yours . . . whether the world to come, or life or death, or the present or the future—all belong to you, and you belong to Christ, and Christ belongs to God" (1 Cor 3:22).

The resurrection does not cancel the Jesus' presence to all creation. He holds everything and everyone in the power of deathless life. He belongs to the whole, containing it in his risen form of life. Into the ambiguity of our death-bound lives is uttered the Word of life. True life is not subject to the power of death and the destructive forces it symbolises: "Christ being raised from the dead will never die again. Death no longer has dominion over him" (Rom 6:9). In his resurrection, Jesus is the final breakthrough in the emergence of the universe. He is the great transformation through which all things are born anew. In the most comprehensive and cosmic sense, all the promises of God find their Yes in him (2 Cor 1:20). Christ has gone before us as "the first born of all creation":

> If the Spirit of him who raised Jesus from the dead dwells in you, he who raised Jesus from the dead will give life to your mortal bodies also through the Spirit who dwells in you (Rom 7:11).

The Way of the Cross becomes in the end a path travelled by the whole universe, a way in which our hearts and minds expand to include everything and everyone in the love we have found revealed. The exultant words of a saintly preacher of fifteen centuries ago leave us today with a question: Is our hope big enough, really worthy of the love that has found us?

Through Christ's resurrection, the underworld is opened; through the neophytes of the Church, the world is renewed; heaven is unlocked through the Holy Spirit. For the underworld is opened and gives back the dead; earth is renewed, and from it springs the crop of those who are risen; heaven is unlocked and receives them as they ascend.

So the good thief ascends to paradise; the bodies of the saints enter the holy city; the dead return to the living; and sharing, as it were, Christ's resurrection, all the elements tend upward . . . By a single process the Saviour's passion raises from the depths, lifts up from the earth, and places on high.

For Christ's resurrection is life for the dead, pardon for sinners, glory for the saints . . .

And so, my brothers and sisters, we ought to rejoice on this holy day. No one should exclude themselves from the general rejoicing because they have sins on their conscience. No one should refuse to take part in the public worship because of the burden of their misdeeds. However great a sinner they may be, on this day they should not despair of pardon, for the privileges granted on this day are great. If a thief was thought worthy of paradise, why should not a Christian be thought worthy of forgiveness?[3]

---

3. From The Sermons of St Maximus of Turin, Sermon 53, 1-2.4, The Divine Office II, the Office of Readings, Fifth Sunday of Eastertide, 580–582.

Toward The Ascension

The ascension draws the believing mind and heart into another realm—never to be clarified until the Lord returns in glory. Despite its inevitable 'open-endedness', it is worth noting that, of all the events, words and actions involved in the mystery of Jesus Christ, the ascension is closest to contemporary believers. In the concrete actuality of Christian existence, the ascended and glorified Christ is faith's point of departure when all that is past, present and still to come is integrated in terms of the one Christ Event. Paradoxically, the effect of the ascension is not to disembody the Lord, but to discern him now present in the fullness of his humanity. Unless it is backlit by Easter radiance, there would be no story to tell and none worth the telling.

There is a tinge of paradox here: the meaning of the ascension is not so much to be found in this or that scriptural passage in the New Testament, but rather, the whole meaning of the New Testament is to be found *within* the ascension. It opens the horizon in which the whole Gospel can be contemplated. A thinking faith needs to allow for the full play of interweaving connections between the ascension and every aspect of God's self-revelation in Christ. Through this expansive and inclusive event, not only is the ascended Christ still incarnate, but we ourselves, as Christian believers, members of the Body of Christ, participate even now in the great transformation that has taken place in the resurrection and ascension of the crucified One. This in no way diminishes the dialogue between faith and science but makes such exchanges more open and imaginative. An 'ascensional' perspective can have a twofold good effect. The 'soul-less body' of materialistic modernity comes up against the transformed materiality and vitality of the cosmic Body of Christ. On the other hand, the "disembodied soul" of a rootless postmodernity meets the body-affirming reality which puts the soul back into its body—in this case, into the Body of Christ in all its relationships. Neither the church nor the eucharist 'contains' Christ, for he is the One in whom all things are contained and are held together (Col 1:17).

Every aspect of Christ's life, death, resurrection, ascension and return in glory continuously interconnect and interpenetrate in the one divine economy of grace at work in every 'now'. Indeed, the completion of Christ's his specific mission means that he is available in every moment, continuing to give himself to each generation of believers.

What the ascension means is illuminated in some measure by the intimate experience of our own bodily existence. 'My body' is not merely a physical object which I 'have' or possess. It is rather the vibrant network of relationships in which I exist in the world. It is not, however, an individual organism enclosed in its own skin, but the matrix of manifold and interrelated dimensions of embodiment found in relation, say, to other human beings, to all living things, and to the earth, the land, time, space and nature. The body-language of the New Testament stretches to differing kinds of corporeal relationships—the sexual, maternal, familial, social, ecological, cosmic. All of these can throw light on the eschatological but expanding reality of the ascended Body of Christ (Eph 4:4).

Jesus incorporates his followers into his Body, throughout history and through the Church—and above all through the Eucharist, as uniquely Christ's bodily self-giving within and for the Church. In the Body of Christ, the natural dimensions of bodily being are transformed in accord with Christ's resurrection and ascension. A new cosmic and theocentric order comes into being. Its field of generative relationships constitutes a new nature, a new principle of action, anticipated in the church's celebration of the eucharist. In the ascended Jesus, time, space, body and nature are refashioned. History, instead of being a concatenation of episodic events, is caught up in the updraught of all things being gathered into Christ to the point when God is 'all in all' (1 Cor 15:28).

This is to say that the ascension is both a movement and an horizon, suggested in the words of Jesus, 'I go to prepare a place for you' (Jn 14:2) in his Father's house of many rooms. He goes on to assure his disciples, 'And if I go and prepare a place for you, I will come again and take you to myself, so that where I am, you may be also' (Jn 14:2-3). The ascension therefore is presented, not as a mythological addition to the story of Jesus, but as the movement and horizon in which God's ingathering action is occurring. From that point of view, Christ's ascension and departure from this world amounts to the making of the Christian heaven. For Jesus ascends, not simply in his individual humanity, but as embodying a world, perfected, transformed, and offered to the Father, and diaphanous with the Light (Rev 21:23).

Christ's ascension is an ending of a previous mode of life, as he vanishes from the visibilities of earthly existence. That invisibility makes quite clear that Church does not possess, control or contain Christ. Rather, a totality is contained by him. Christ is not 'in' in the sacraments, just as he is not 'in' the world. Rather, elements of the world—the bread and wine, oil, water, and so on—are, through the action of the Spirit, assumed 'into Christ', transfigured by him as anticipations of the new creation—so to become the sacraments of faith. The sacramental economy, being permanent, is guaranteed in the efficacy of its communication of the grace of Christ's presence. This is different from the episodic and privileged appearances of the risen Christ over the forty-day period. The time of the sacraments has no end as long as history continues.

Through the ascension Christ rises above history, but not as a flight from it, but to give history a new density and direction. It is not simply biological time (with its aging and entropy), but the time of an ever broader and deeper realisation of our true selves in the Body of Christ. Time in Christ has entered into the trinitarian eternity of loving exchange. Its flow and direction remains so that the interpersonal communion existing between the Father and the Son can be extended to all ages, from one generation to the next (Jn 17:20-24).

All this is to say that the ascension does not take Christ out of time, but is the condition for his complete immersion in it, as its fullness. Faith is the consciousness of having time 'in him', so that he becomes the measure and goal of time. If time is 'the measure of motion' (Aristotle), the Body of Christ is the fullest measure of what is truly moving in history and in the universe itself. Jesus in his ascent to the Father brings time to its redemptive completion. In this 'time after the ascension' when the church believes without seeing, Christ is more perfectly present in each 'now' than could ever have been the case in his earthly life.

We have already mentioned that ascension pervades the New Testament in different ways and in different contexts (*cf* Lk 24:50–53, Acts 2:30–35; Jn 20:17; Mk 16:19; Eph 4:8–10; 1 Tim 3:16; Heb 4:14; 9:27). There is a dialectic of presence and absence, of seeing and non-seeing, that can never be resolved on this side of the Parousia. Faith 'looks back' over the whole life and mission of Jesus; and from which, we 'look forward' into the life and mission of the Church. The retrospective view entails the recognition of Christ as the individual Jesus of Nazareth. The prospective view recognises the living, present reality of the crucified and risen Jesus as the Christ—and the fulfilment that is promised. More precisely, the history of Christian consciousness contains a recollection of both an economy of post-resurrection appearances of Jesus, and their ending (1 Cor 15:3–11). But this ending leads into the time of his ascension in which Jesus lives as the conqueror of death, and as embodying the new creation which will be fully realised with his return at the end of history.

In his ascension, Christ departs into the indefinability of the realm of God from which the Spirit, the other Paraclete, will come (Jn 16:7). If Jesus has remained under the conditions of the previous economy, if he had not ascended to the incalculable realm from which all comes as sheer gift, the receptivity and unreserved character of faith would be compromised. But the ascension of Jesus makes 'heaven' the realm from which the Spirit—the gift preceding and crowning all gifts—is given. The life of the world to come is not a human production or a worldly resource, but the gift from 'on high', and incalculable gift of the Spirit, breathing where it will (Jn 3:8). In the Pauline idiom, the ascension means not only that Christ fills all things but also that he is the source of all gifts necessary for the building up of his Body (*cf* Eph 4:7–11). As gifts abound from the realm to which Christ has ascended. So too does thanksgiving and serene longing for the promised return of Christ (*cf* Jn 16:7; 16:24; 17:13). There is no desire to cling to the past as if faith were an endless reconfiguration of the recorded memories of Jesus of Nazareth within the dimensions of the present world (Jn 20:17). For Paul, 'the human point of view' is a horizontal perspective on Jesus untroubled by the vertical disruption of his resurrection and ascension (2 Cor 5:16). Only an horizon enlarged by faith in the resurrection and ascension of Jesus can appreciate that Christ embodies 'a new creation: everything old has passed away' (2 Cor 5:17).

With the ascension of Jesus into the cloud of divine glory, there will indeed a 'cloud of unknowing'—sufficient to justify the vast and varied tradition of the *via negativa*. But from out of this absence, this negation, this darkness of familiar knowledge with its fixed bearings and clear outlines, Christ will appear, as the fulfilment of all our knowing and hoping. But he does not come as an idea, but in his personal identity, indeed, as the Word Incarnate *in person* and in the universal outreach of his identity.

To summarise: the crucified Jesus died and was buried—and remains dead to this life and its world. Yet he has risen from the dead into another order of existence, and disclosed himself alive in another realm to chosen witnesses. This mode of self-disclosure was episodic, and with the ascension of the risen One to the right hand of the Father, this privileged mode of seeing came to an end. Blessedness now consisted in *believing* rather than in *seeing* Jesus, either in terms of his previous human existence in the world, or in the mode of privileged episodic encounters after the resurrection. Indeed, the ascension Christ in terms of the divine economy of salvation means that he is 'out of sight'—in the way that God is out of sight, even though the Holy Spirit is sent and Jesus' promise to return remains.

In that respect, questions about the ascension, the Body of Christ, and materiality of creation[1] have already demanded some reference to the Catholic doctrine of the Assumption of Our Lady, solemnly defined in 1950. This is one more point where, theologically speaking, the intentionality of faith has hurried past its powers of expression. If Mary is declared to be assumed, body and soul, into heaven, then the corporate, historical authority of the Catholic Church is thereby committed to a view of materiality, corporeality, and physicality in a way that is largely beyond our powers of expression, in either conceptual or even imaginative terms. Here we can do little more than note that it would be of great ecumenical significance if our understandings of the ascension of Christ and the assumption of Mary interacted more positively. In the concrete liturgical unfolding of Catholic tradition, the ascension of Jesus would be deprived of its salvific significance if unrelated to the assumption of Mary as cause to effect. Likewise, the assumption, if more clearly connected to the ascension of Christ, would have a clearer ecclesiological and cosmic

---

1. Bulgakov, *The Lamb of God,* 393–98.

significance. In both cases, faith stretches forward and upward. Ambrose of Milan expressed the cosmic sweep of the mystery of Christ with the words, 'In Christ's resurrection, the world arose. In Christ's resurrection, the heavens arose; in Christ's resurrection the earth itself arose'.[2] We have emphasised the significance of the ascension as the completion and expansion of incarnation; and that enables us to glimpse the connections between the incarnation, the ascension and the universal transformation anticipated in the Catholic doctrine of Mary 'assumed body and soul into heaven'. In such a context, the assumption of Mary is a concrete symbol of the overbrimming significance of the ascension itself. Now assumed into the glory of Christ, she is the anticipation of the heaven of a transfigured creation. In that regard, Mary is the paradigmatic instance of creation open to, collaborating with, and transformed by, the creative mystery of God in Christ. As the mother of Christ, she symbolises the generativity of creation under the power of the Spirit. In her, as the Advent antiphon has it, 'the earth has been opened to bud forth the Saviour'. In its confession of the assumption, Christian hope finds a particular confirmation. In Mary, now assumed body and soul into the heaven of God and Christ, our humanity, our world and even our history have reached their divinely-destined term. She embodies the reality of our world as having received into itself the mystery that is to transform the universe in its entirety.

Mary of Nazareth is the name of an historical person—the mother of Jesus. Yet history has no record of her life except through the documents of faith, above all the Gospels of the New Testament. It is significant in the present context that she has become known to faith only through the immense transformation that took place in the resurrection and ascension of her Son, and its impact on human consciousness through faith, hope and love. The assumption enables faith to glimpse the 'opened heaven' of Jesus' promise to the disciples in his conversation with Nathanael: 'Amen, amen, I say to you, you will see heaven opened and the angels of God ascending and descending on the Son of Man' (Jn 1:51). Her Son embodies the open heaven of communication between God and creation.

To detach the Ascension of Christ from the Assumption of Mary would leave it without its most personal effect. Furthermore, if the

---

2. *De excessu fratris sui*, bk 1. *PL* 16, 1354.

assumption of Mary is left disconnected from the ascension of Christ, it can quickly become a devotional 'optional extra', and cease to be carrier of the universal and cosmic transformation of all creation in Christ. On the other hand, in the light of the ascension in which the presence and activity of Christ is viewed, belief in the assumption of the mother of Christ, body and soul, into heaven cannot but continue to inspire a fresh hearing of this exhortation from the Letter to the Ephesians,

> So if you have been raised with Christ, seek the things that are above, where Christ is seated at the right hand of God. Set your minds on the things that are above, not on things that are on earth, for you have died, and your life is hidden with Christ in God. When Christ who is your life is revealed, then you will be revealed with him in glory (Eph 3:1–4).

Two further points: first, by conceiving of the ascension in its relationship to the expanding event of the incarnation, we preclude the tendency to think of the ascension as Christ's disembodiment, dehumanisation or 'excarnation'. The continuance and expansion of the incarnation, when so understood, has profound ecclesiological and eschatological significance. Secondly, not only is the incarnation conceived of as an expanding event, but the meaning of the embodiment emerges in a world and in the Church—the Body of Christ. The phenomenon of existing and communicating in the body suggested a range of analogical applications to the transformed bodiliness of Christ, his embodiment in the Church and his communication to it through the sacraments, and the eucharist above all.

Because of the ascension, elemental notions such as 'world', 'heaven', 'time' and 'place' need to be recast. If Christ has ascended in his humanity into heaven, then humanity and the world in which it is inextricably immersed has entered into a new mode of existence. It is not as though Christ has left the world, but is related to it a new way—just our humanity has not been discarded in the ascended Christ. In this sense, heaven, in Christian terms, is not a vague celestial location but communion with God in Christ in a creation transformed. It is, in the words of Jesus in John's Gospel, 'the opened heaven', with 'the angels of God ascending and descending upon the Son of Man' (Jn 1:51). Through Christ's ascension to the Father, a new age of communication between God and the world is inaugurated. In Christ, the world has been irreversibly taken up into the life of God, and God has come down into the life of the world. As has been emphasised on previous occasions, it is no longer a matter of fitting Christ into an unredeemed world or seeing him disappear into a vaguely determined heaven. Rather, the challenge consists in seeing both the world and heaven embodied in him: something new has begun; time and space are newly configured when the ascended Christ is the centre and the focus of God's action—and theological exploration.

A refreshed sense of Christ as the transcendent and indefinably all-inclusive Other is a powerful stimulus to dialogue. In the wide world of divine creation, and in the boundless dimensions of God's heaven to which Christ has ascended, he is not contained but adored and named as the Lord of all creation to the glory of the Father (Phil 2:10–11). Unconstrained by any mundane condition, Christ must be left free to act and to give in ways always hidden to human comprehension. He is ascended . . .

The Glory of God

There is a wondrous description in the Book of Chronicles of how the Ark of the Covenant was brought to Solomon's newly constructed Temple. We are told on a couple of occasions how this sense of the divine presence was so strong that the impressive priestly gathering, assembled in all its respective choral, orchestral and ceremonial ministries, could not perform its duties: '. . . the house of the Lord was filled with a cloud, so that the priests could not stand to minister because of the cloud; for the glory of the Lord filled the house of God' (2 Chron 5:13–14, 7:1–2).

That, you might say, would have been a good problem to have– at least as we understand things in these latter days when 'organised religion' is not highly regarded. We could cope with such a positively disabling manifestation of God's glory. To be confronted by the awe-inspiring presence of God, to be so drawn out of ourselves in the experience of the divine glory, this would surely be preferable to religious 'business as usual'. It is not unlikely that we would like God to show a bit more glory!

But where has this glory gone? Are we looking in the right direction? And another niggling question: Would we recognise it if we saw it? Some future judgment might find that our that our celebrity-crazed age has been largely blinded to the true radiance of God's glory.

In a general sense, 'glory' seems to be one of those basic notions that can never be satisfactorily pinned down in precise definition. It implies a recognition of what, in the end, is most-prized. In this regard, it is the felt radiance of a life's fullest meaning and achievement. It is linked to the notion of reputation, and being held in the highest regard by others and the public esteem that follows. In that situation of social esteem, a person is identified as the author of some remarkable achievement. His or her name will live on. For the glorious one has 'made a name', and is celebrated in a mythic forever for deeds of splendor. One way or another, glory is a death-defying quality. Glory stands against the erosion of time, countering the power of death to annul and diminish the human good, as the classic literatures of the world attest.

Paradoxically, dying for a noble cause is more often than not the price of glory and the 'immortality' it promises. Whatever glory means, it is apt to provoke a lot of questions. What, for instance, most secures and enhances one's personal identity? In the assessment of our worth, whose judgment most counts? How can life defy death? And, most fundamentally, who is the 'god'– if any– who glorifies us, or who is glorified by us.

This is where John's Gospel is of special interest. It is quite direct in distinguishing two radically opposed forms of glory even though the same Greek word, *doxa* (translating the Hebrew *kabod*) is used. Only in the Bible does the same word mean both the social acknowledgment of one's reputation and role, and the unique saving revelation of God. The evangelist, puzzling over the failure of 'the Jews' to accept Jesus (note that 'the Jews' was a term frequently used for those who most violently oppose the Gospel, though all were Jews–including Jesus– in a more general sense). John comments, 'They loved human glory more than the glory that comes from God' (Jn 12:43). Jesus had previously asked his adversaries, 'How can you believe when you accept glory from one another and do not seek the glory that comes from the one who alone is God?' (5:44).

In the perspective of the Gospel, the world is in the thrall of false glory, closing it against the true glory that is being revealed (*Cf* Jn 5:41–44; 9:24; 12:43; 16:2; 1 Jn 2:15–17). Though this false glory may well speak appreciatively of God's glory, it is way off the mark when it works to remove both Jesus and his followers from the scene. Jesus, addressing his disciples, makes an unsettling prediction: 'They will put you out of the synagogues. Indeed, an hour is coming when those who kill you will think that by doing so 'they are offering worship to God. And they will do this because they have not known the Father or me' (Jn 16:2–3).

In subversive contrast to the world's idea of glory is the life-giving glory of God. It will climactically shine forth in the self-giving of Jesus on the Cross. In the light of that final disclosure, the life and deeds of the Son would be interpreted as the unveiling of the glory of God: 'And we have seen his glory, the glory of the Father's only Son, full of grace and truth' (1:14). In the light of God's true glory, the disciples, hitherto affected by a worldly notion of glory, began to see things quite differently: 'His disciples did not understand these things at first; but when Jesus was glorified, then they remembered that these things had been written of him and had been done to him (12:16). God's glory shines out through the Cross. As Jesus gives himself for the life of the world, the forces of worldly glory are annulled: 'Now is the judgment of this world; now the ruler of this world will be driven out. And I, when I am lifted up from the earth, will draw all people to myself' (Jn 12:31-32; see also 13:31; 14:13; 15:8; 16:14; 17:1, 5, 22, 24).

There is one unsettling point in all this. Seeing and witnessing to God's glory seems to be linked to a rather disreputable status in the worldly glory Faith in Christ does not lead to a glorious reputation. The gift of faith, of recognizing 'the only true God' (Jn 17:3), brings a special vulnerability. God's glory is counter-cultural, when the culture's notion of glory is counter-God—or, more usually, 'antichrist' (1 Jn 2:18). The dynamics of worldly glory and human respect numb the heart's capacity to recognise God's glory (Jn 5:41–44; 7:18; 8:15; 12:43). The 'ruler of this world' is terminally antagonistic to the glory of the Cross (Jn 13:27; 14:30; 16:11; 17:12; 1 Jn 5:19). A culture intent on securing its glory through vengeance and domination is not hospitable to what is not of the world (Jn 8:40, 44; 10:31; 11:50; 12:10; 16:2-3; 1 Jn 3:11-15). The recognition of God's glory is impossible where idols reign (Jn 5:37b).

The Paraclete comes to contend against the self-justifying stratagems of worldly glory (Jn 16:8–11). The 'opened heaven' (Jn 1:51) of communion with God that Jesus promised, his commandment of love, and his gifts of truth, joy, peace and life to the full (Jn 14:15–27) are in stark contrast to the way of the world (1 Jn 2:15–18). It would seem that God reveals his glory only to those who, under pressure from the gods of the dominant culture, are prepared to make a stand of practical adoration of the one true God. Worshiping the Father 'in spirit and in truth' (Jn 4:23–24), they are engaged in an ongoing struggle to keep themselves from idols (1 Jn 5:21).

The world of human glory will inflict death on the Son; but the glory of God will be an epiphany of love enacted in that death. On the one side, death is inflicted on Jesus in the interests of human glory. On the other, glory of God is revealed in that self-surrendering death on the Cross. It leaves faith wondering—and perhaps fearing—what the glory of God and glorification by God might mean.

Still, the Gospel invites believers to witness to God's glory through a transformation of mind and heart that will make them contest all other notions of glory. This will not make them popular; indeed, challenged in its glory, the world will hate them (Jn 15:18–20). Nonetheless, through the Cross of Jesus, the glory of self-giving love, the true form of life everlasting is disclosed. In 'seeing his glory' (Jn 1:14), the hearts of believers open to an horizon in which life can be lived in its deathless glory, in undying communion with God. Faith reaches into the glory and the love which Jesus enjoyed from the Father 'before the foundation of the world' (Jn17:5, 24). The realm of glory is disclosed as the sphere of self-giving love, the absolute reality of 'the truth that will make you free' (Jn 8:32). In that realm of glory, love is the decisive life-value, 'for God is love' (1 Jn 4:8).

Where, then, is the glory of God? As the antiphon for Holy Thursday sings, *Ubi Caritas et amor, Deus ibi est*- 'Wherever there is charity and love, there too is God'. Where there is love for one's neighbour and even for one's enemies, wherever there is compassion for the poor, solidarity with the defenceless and resistance to the murderous idols that govern so much of the world's business, there, the glory of God is revealed. And the priests 'cannot go about their business'. Why note admit that that we are not always looking in the right direction.

Milton Keynes UK
Ingram Content Group UK Ltd.
UKHW030057270724
446175UK00004B/119